Little
Laureates
2008

Verses From Yorkshire
Edited by Donna Samworth

Young Writers

First published in Great Britain in 2008 by:
Young Writers
Remus House
Coltsfoot Drive
Peterborough
PE2 9JX
Telephone: 01733 890066
Website: www.youngwriters.co.uk

SB ISBN 978-1 84431 648 9

Foreword

Young Writers was established in 1991 and has been passionately devoted to the promotion of reading and writing in children and young adults ever since. The quest continues today. Young Writers remains as committed to the nurturing of poetic and literary talent as ever.

This year's Young Writers competition has proven as vibrant and dynamic as ever and we are delighted to present a showcase of the best poetry from across the UK and in some cases overseas. Each poem has been selected from a wealth of *Little Laureates 2008* entries before ultimately being published in this, our seventeenth primary school poetry series.

Once again, we have been supremely impressed by the overall quality of the entries we have received. The imagination, energy and creativity which has gone into each young writer's entry made choosing the poems a challenging and often difficult but ultimately hugely rewarding task - the general high standard of the work submitted ensured this opportunity to bring their poetry to a larger appreciative audience.

We sincerely hope you are pleased with this final collection and that you will enjoy *Little Laureates 2008 Verses From Yorkshire* for many years to come.

Contents

Bethany Fox (10)   11
Sophie Crump (9)   11
Summer Wagstaffe (9)   11
Lucy Bagnall (10)   12
Lucy Callaghan (10)   13
Emily Cartwright (10)   14
Sarah Simpson (10)   15
Amber Cowan (9)   16
Charlotte Carter (11)   17
Olivia Oldfield (8)   17
Chloe Davis (10)   18
Harry Seaman (10)   18
Katherine Leflay (10)   19
Eleanor Johnson (9)   19
Charlotte Ward (9)   20

Gilamoor CE Primary School

Harry Holt (9)   20
Bethany Haughton (11)   21
Faye Nicholson (11)   21
Bethany Flinton (8)   22
Daisy Robbins (11)   22
Matthew Hellowell (8)   23
Owen Hayhurst (8)   23
Joe Robbins (9)   24
Billie Cheney (8)   24
Leah Preston (10)   25
Erin Nicholson (7)   25
Ruaraidh McGill (10)   26

Hucklow Primary School

Lena Abdurub (8)   26
Musaid Saleh (8)   27
James Lacey (8)   27
Patrick Collins (8)   27
Mona Shaibi (7)   28

Hyrstmount Junior School

Jumainah Saiyed (10)   28
Saad Daji (9)   28

Mahdiyya Malek (8)   29
Nabilah Kathrada (7)   29
Aadam Patel (9)   29
Abdullah Mamaniat (7)   30
Saudah Chopdat (8)   30
Mohammed Hashim Ravat (9)   30
Aarifah Seedat (8)   31
Muhammed Laher (9)   31
Maryam Chothia (8)   31
Fatimah Popat (9)   32
Maaria Bahadur (8)   32
Ebrahim Momoniat (8)   32
Rokeya Karolia (8)   33
Maariya Rafiq (8)   33
Tasneem Badat (8)   33
Amina Rawat (11)   34
Unaysah Daji (11)   34
Faatimah Patel (10)   35
Daanyaal Qadeer (7)   35
Sumaiyah Chopdat (9)   36

Ingleby Arncliffe Primary School
Catherine Bailey (9)   36
Helen Bailey (9)   37
Granville Cornforth (10)   37
Eric Hillary (10)   38
Adam Wren (9)   38
Angus MacColl (10)   39
Tom Rudd (9)   39
Alex Barlow (10)   39
Billie Godley (9)   40
Holly Calder (10)   41

Ings Primary School
Charlie Holborn   41
Emma Cowell (11)   42
Georgia Mullin-Kipling (11)   42
Luke Welford (9)   43
Chloe Edwards (11)   43
Chloe Foley (9)   44
Victoria Johnson (10)   44

Louella Sumpton (9)	45
Kai Weymes (10)	45
Leonna Foley (10)	46
Tegan Cooper (10)	46
Bradley Williams (9)	47
Caitlan Taylor (9)	47
Georgia Carter (10)	48
Charlotte Cook (9)	48
Ashley Fill (11)	49
Enya Horton (11)	49
Ellie Taylor (9)	50
Jasmine North (8)	50
Abby Forrester (8)	50
Gagandeep Manota (8)	51
Grant William Marshall (11)	51
Leah Robinson (8)	51
Elizabeth Pickering (8)	52
Abbie Everett (8)	52
Lauren Gledson (9)	52
Megan Pleasance (7)	53
Daisy Fletcher (8)	53
Marcus Watson (8)	53
Jasmine Jade Rushworth (8)	54
Ellie Barnett (7)	54
Cathy Yeung (8)	54
Terrileigh Johnson (7)	55
Amy Carmichael (8)	55
Grace Stevenson (8)	55
Ellie-Mae Wakes (8)	56
Bethany Symes (8)	56

Maltby Lilly Hall Junior School

Alfie Porter (9)	56
Lauren Day (9)	57
Ben Cliff (8)	57
Jake Bunting (9)	57
Francesca Riley (9)	58
Mark Higham (9)	58
Ben Ferguson (9)	58
Aidan Hazell (9)	58
Shannon Long (9)	59

Natasha Connell (8)   59
Jack Davies (9)   59
Jack Belcher (9)   60
Bradley Callum Marshall (8)   60
Jordan Wright (8)   60
Lucy Tune (9)   61
Rachel Kittle   61
Libby Barlow (8)   61
Megan Williams (8)   61
Declan Hewitt (8)   62

North & South Cowton Primary School
Jonathan Parr (10)   62
Jack Walmsley (8)   62
James Armstrong (10)   63
Maisie Imogen Price (10)   63
Thomas James Lockwood (9)   63
Carl Hughes (9)   64

Oakhill Primary School
Leah Smith (9)   64
Caitlin Franklin (8)   64
Mathilda Bassnett (8)   65
Joshua Massey (9)   65
Tom Sanders (8)   65
Jessica Fox (9)   65
Jack Lawton (9)   66
Thomas Speed (9)   66
Jessica Wright (8)   66
Leah Harston (9)   67
Christopher David Holling (9)   67

Our Lady of Sorrows Catholic Primary School
Ruairi Lowe (8)   68
Jack Reeve (9)   68
Mitchell Monaghan (8)   69
Jessica Hassall (9)   69
Oliver Newbert (10)   70
Amy Fudge (8)   70
Joseph Pinkney (9)   71
Ciara Batty (8)   71

Emily Kirkbride (9)   72
Aaron Hartin (10)   72
Emma Hinchliffe (8)   72

Rosedale Abbey Primary School
Lydia Coote (8)   73
Chloe Marley (8)   73
Bethany Richardson (8)   73
Cara Blackburne-Brace (8)   74
Maddie Kenderdine (10)   74
Liam Thompson (7)   74
Olivia Doughty (9)   75
Annabelle Horseman (11)   75
Bethany Thompson (7)   75
Thomas Middleton (11)   76

St Olaves School, York
Alice Gilman (8)   76
Polly Moss (9)   77
Natasha Bell (9)   77

Serlby Park School
Emma Thompson (11)   78
Gemma Rodger (9)   79
Morgan Kane (9)   80
Katy Halbert (10)   80
Shannon Smith (11)   80
Thomas Michael Maule (9)   81
Callum Rudd (11)   81
Benjamin Oxley (10)   81
Jade Lyons (10)   82

Sitwell Junior School
Ben Bishop (9)   82
Edward Spink (10)   83
Mariam Hussain (8)   83
Alexandra Marrison (8)   84
Rachael Hill (9)   84
Isobel Hancock (8)   84

Lewis Waters (11) 85
Georgia Barnard (9) 85
Kyle Allen (8) 85
Leanne Davis (11) 86
Gary Foster (11) 86
Jennifer Howsego (10) 87
William Morgan (11) 87
William Bladon (10) 88
Ellie Hancock & Pippa Humphries (10) 88
Georgia O'Brien (8) 89
Lewis Gee (8) 89
April Ogden (7) 89
Matthew Brookes (8) 90
Natty McKenzie-Smith (8) 90
Amelia Davis (8) 90
Abbie Ollivant (8) 91
Charlotte Hunter (7) 91
Michael Rose (9) 91
Thomas Woolley (8) 92
Kay Russell (9) 92
Matthew Bailey (9) 92
Maddie Shellcock (10) 93

Sutton Park Primary School
George Bean & Matthew Aistrop (10) 94

Tickton CE Primary School, Beverley
Tom Marton (10) 94
Hetty Jackson & Ellie Shingles (10) 95
James Woods (9) 95
Christopher Foster (10) 96
Lauren Wilson (10) 97
Megan Selway (11) 98
Connor Ashby (10) 99
Lewis Pritchard (9) 100
Rachel Stanforth (10) 100
Victoria Kirbitson (11) 101
Jessica Chew (8) 101
Evie Guttridge (9) 102
Jack Head (8) 102

Wellington Primary School

The Poems

My Dream

My dream is turquoise and shiny.
My dream tastes like biscuits.
My dream smells like strawberries.
My dream looks like lavender.
My dream sounds like the merry-go-round music.
My dream feels like a pillow.

Anya Newell (7)

Cancer

Cancer is tragic
There may be no cure
But with a little bit of magic
We'll put an end to it I'm sure.

Loads of different diseases to catch
But we can hatch this wonderful plan.
What's better, waiting now or later?
To stop this I know we can.

Rebekah Wootton (10)

Tornadoes

Tornadoes
A tornado is near
You'd better beware
Destroying hotels,
Breaking houses,
Smashing cars,
Still as death.
Smashing, crashing,
Hissing, screaming,
Strong, invincible,
Powerful,
Sucking,
Twirling,
Tornadoes.

Craig Hardie (9)
Alanbrooke Primary School

Embarrassment

It sounds like a thousand people laughing at me.
It tastes like a burnt apple that's just come out of the oven.
It looks like a chipmunk biting my fingers.
It feels like you're trapped in a tube and there's no way to get out.
It reminds me of the smell of rotten eggs.

Megan Nagy (9)
Aston Lodge Primary School

Embarrassment

It sounds like a radio buzzing.
It tastes like bleeding gums.
It looks like squashed tomatoes.
It feels like beating drums.
It reminds me of a first kiss.

Emma Allen (8)
Aston Lodge Primary School

Embarrassment

It sounds like a car alarm in my stomach.
It tastes like rotten eggs.
It looks like a tomato being squished.
It feels like butterflies in my stomach.
It reminds me of blood.
When you get embarrassed you blush, your face goes as red as blood
Or when you do a handstand.

Georgia Nowlan (8)
Aston Lodge Primary School

Love

Love is beautiful.
Love is special.
Love is God.
Most of all love is special to me and everyone I know
Love is nice.

Abbie Duncan (9)
Aston Lodge Primary School

Embarrassment

What does it sound like?
It sounds like a big crash.
What does it taste like?
Some dog food.
What does it look like?
It looks like an old cat has just been dumped
What does it reminds you of?
It reminds me of my first day at school.

Connor Atkinson (9)
Aston Lodge Primary School

Greed

Greed is bad, it makes people sad.
Greed sounds like people munching away at your favourite food.
Greed tastes like coffee with lumps of mushrooms in it.
Greed looks like fat monsters walking towards you.
Greed feels like holding your favourite teddy bear broken in your hands.
Greed reminds me of people fighting over something
                                                    and it getting broken.
Greed puts a tear into someone's eye.

Olivia Hamlet (9)
Aston Lodge Primary School

In The Inner Core

In the inner core it is hotter than a summer's day
It sounds like lava bubbling like a giant bubble wrap and rocks clashing
together.
No man has ever lived to see the inner core.

Thomas Coxon (8)
Aston Lodge Primary School

Dark

It sounds like owls tweeting in the night sky.
It tastes like air coming into your mouth and down your lungs.
It looks like outer space in the deep, deep dark.
It feels like cold and damp.
It reminds me of spooky caves.

Lauren Senior (8)
Aston Lodge Primary School

School

School is fun, you can run
You have got people to look after you at half-past two.
What would happen at the end of the day when everyone
has gone home?
While everyone is playing on their phone,
Who knows what would happen at school,
While everyone is at home in their swimming pool.
School is fun, you can run.

Carla Leigh (8)
Aston Lodge Primary School

Embarrassment

It sounds like a nail scraping down a chalk board.
It tastes like squashed tomatoes.
It looks like people laughing at you.
It feels like you have been hit.
It reminds me of my birthday song.

Brandon Sykes (8)
Aston Lodge Primary School

Dancing In The Air

U nicorns are everywhere, dancing in the air
N ow they are here and there
I n and out of the sky they fly
C ome with me to see my friend Kye
O ver a cloud, a smell drifts by
R un with the wind, please try
N ice is the best word they know
S o watch them glow.

Courtney Wade (9)
Aston Lodge Primary School

Embarrassment

Embarrassment looks like you've eaten a red-hot chilli.
Embarrassment smells like mouldy cheese.
Embarrassment tastes like mouldy bread.
Embarrassment feels like no one is on your side.
Embarrassment reminds me of butterflies in your stomach.

Morgan Locking (8)
Aston Lodge Primary School

Death Eaters

The blood is cold.
The guts are slimy and the eyes are like a bite of flesh.
The heart is bumping and the bones are juicy.
The vines are purple-blooded.
The blood vessels are like electric wires.

Jorden Busby (8)
Aston Lodge Primary School

Love Poem

L ove is God, God is great.
O ver the hills and over the hay
V ibration, vibration, everyone feels vibration
E veryone is God's child, children are great.

Jack Gibson (9)
Aston Lodge Primary School

The Earth's Inner Core

Bubbling lava big and bold
Shooting up through life's cold core
Through the hot core, through the gems
Up the volcano, where will it end?

Jacob Randle (8)
Aston Lodge Primary School

Embarrassment

It sounds like a pin dropping on the ground.
It tastes like gone off apples.
It looks like people laughing all around me.
It feels like butterflies in my tummy.
It reminds me of my first kiss.

Meaghan Walker (8)
Aston Lodge Primary School

Books

Books about wonders far and wide,
Books about thunder that makes me hide.
Books about dogs that dig in the dirt,
Books about frogs that like to hurt.
Books about cats that like to scratch,
Books about bats that have their own patch.
Books about castles very tall,
Books about hassles in a long, long hall.
Books about dancing like never before,
Books about prancing around the floor.
I love reading all these things,
I like reading about everything.

India Fairie (8)
Boynton Primary School

Good Books

I went to the library to have a look
And I found a pile of good books.
Books of dark nights and of great heights
Books of good times
And of riddles and rhymes.
To find all of these things in a book
The library is where you need to look.

John Storey (8)
Boynton Primary School

What I Like

I really don't like cabbage
But my dad says it does you good.
I always spit it out,
I say I'd rather have some pud!

I really don't like sprouts
But my dad says they do you good.
When I say I don't like them
He always says I should.

My dad doesn't like cheese
But I say it does you good.
He says he doesn't like it,
I say he really should!

Abigail Blackford (8)
Boynton Primary School

If I Had Wings

If I had wings I could touch the moon
I could touch the planets, I could touch the stars
If I had wings I could look down on planets
I could look down on trees
I could look down on the park.

Nathaniel Watson (8)
Boynton Primary School

Softer

Softer than a feather from a baby bird
Softer than a pillow from my comfy bed
Softer than a newborn lamb leaping high in spring
Softer than a velvet cushion on a princess' chair
Softer than a sponge in my relaxing bath.

Georgia Smelt (8)
Boynton Primary School

Flowers

I planted seeds in a row, in two weeks they started to grow.
My flowers had lovely petals but they were surrounded
by horrible nettles.
I went outside to pull up the weeds, water is now what my flowers need.
I looked outside at all the flowers, do they have magical powers?

Megan Thompson (8)
Boynton Primary School

Cats

If I were a cat I would lay down flat
I will creep along the wall or stretch my back tall.
I'd leap up in the air without a care
To catch my tea just for me.

Charlie Dennison (7)
Boynton Primary School

When I Wake Up

I wake up to . . .
Birds tweeting,
Cars beeping,
Dogs sleeping
Cats leaping,
Dogs woofing,
Mum's huffing.

Yasmin Nelson (7)
Boynton Primary School

Mothers

Mothers are on the go day and night
Mothers are always dressed up bright
Mothers are kind
Mothers are never left behind.

Charlotte Slater **(9)**
Boynton Primary School

The Wide Piper Of Hamlet

One day in Hamlet no one was around
Until they heard the most unusual sound.
A short fat girl walked over the hill
It gave the townsfolk a real big thrill.
She wore the most unusual clothes
And where she came from nobody knows.
'I am the Wide Piper and I heard your trouble,
I heard about the real big bubble.'
She made it go to some other place
Then left without a single trace.

Laura Tattershall **(9)**
Brook House Junior School

Flowers

I see daffodils and daisies as I dance in the fields
Lilies and leaves who dance on the wind
Butterflies and bluebells lie on the ground
Roses like rubies sway in the breeze.

Katie Bradley **(7)**
Brook House Junior School

Hallowe'en

Witches flying in the sky, flying so very high
Making a potion, a really smelly lotion
Stirring up trouble, hubble and bubble.
They take all the candy from Mandy
Every Hallowe'en, they make me scream, they are so mean.

Bethany Fox (10)
Brook House Junior School

The Beach

The sea was rough
The wind was tough
And the beach was empty and cool.
The family's leader would be a fool
To walk on the beach with the wind so cruel.
But they walked on the sand, hand in hand
Mum, Dad, sister, brother
All looking after each other
And do you know what they saw from afar?
A rainbow.

Sophie Crump (9)
Brook House Junior School

A Dolphin

A dolphin has blue fins
Like shiny silver tins
Their bodies shine like the dark blue sky
Like bluebirds when they fly
When they swim in the deep blue sea
What a wonderful place it could be
When they flip and dive about
Listen to the seagulls scream and shout.

Summer Wagstaffe (9)
Brook House Junior School

Little Red And The Big Bad Wolf

There once was a little girl who had brown curly hair
Who was off to find her mum at the fair.
Little Red saw Mum gorging on candyfloss
After she finished she put on more lipgloss.
Her mummy said, 'Your grandma has got the flu
Right now, she's probably throwing up down the loo!
I need you to take her these pills and brandy
After, ask her if she is feeling dandy.'

So off Little Red went
Skipping all the way through Kent.
So when she saw the local playground
There wasn't a peep or a sound.
That's because a wolf was nearby,
In the distance she could just hear a baby cry.
Suddenly the wolf came and ran at her,
She could feel the warm soft fur.
'Where are you going?' the bad wolf asked,
As little Red hurried on past.
Never talk to strangers, Little Red thought.
As the wolf questioned, 'What have you brought?'
'I have things to make my grandma feel better,
I have also brought her a get well letter.'
'To get there quicker go through the woods,' the wolf said
Thinking to himself, *she will soon be dead.*

Off Little Red ran into the wood
Running as fast as she could.
Off Mr Wolf went to Grandma's house
Creeping in as quiet as a mouse.
Up the stairs he did go
Climbing each one carefully, very slow.
Fast asleep Grandma was in her bed,
When suddenly the wolf bit off her head!
Brushing and curling his furry head
Then quickly dressing he climbed in bed.
'Oh Grandma, it's very dark in here.'
'Sit by the bed and then you'll be near.'
'Oh Grandma, what big ears you have got.'
'Yes dear, they help me hear a lot.'

'Oh Grandma, you have very big eyes.'
'Yes dear they help me when making the pies.'
'Grandma, your teeth are so sharp and full of goo.'
'Yes dear that's so they can eat *you!*'
One big swallow and Little Red was no more
Then a loud knock banged on the door.
The huntsman stepped inside
He climbed up the stairs in one big stride.
'Spit them out you greedy thing!'
Then with his axe the huntsman started to swing.
Off he chopped the bad wolf's head
Then the wolf was really dead.
Out of the wolf Little Red and Grandma climbed
On hot wolf pies all four of them dined.
Two days later, Little Red could be seen
Wearing a lovely fur coat looking like a queen.

Lucy Bagnall (10)
Brook House Junior School

My Friend Star

I have a friend, she's not from Earth
She told me her name and her date of birth.
She plays at night and not in the day
And she likes to do things in her own little way.

She can make things move with a long stare
And she loves to play with her monstrous bear.
She likes to sit on the garden chair
And comb her tangled long green hair.

She knows what you're thinking; she can read your mind,
She looks like a human but she's none of the kind.
I have a friend, she's not from Earth
Her name is Star, 2040 is her date of birth.

Lucy Callaghan (10)
Brook House Junior School

School!

School is a place where you watch and learn
And loads of writing too,
But most things are quite interesting
Although there's lots of work to do.

Some people like English and maths,
Though, I really love art.
However, I do really well in my maths test
So you can't say I'm not smart.

PE is great,
It is really fun.
I really enjoy netball,
Especially when we're out in the sun.

Lunchtime is the *best*
We need to take a break,
We're all so hungry now
So let us eat *for goodness sake*.

History is really interesting,
Tudors, Egyptians and the war,
And loads more facts that you will want to hear
Also the Romans, how much more?

I really like music
It is one of the best,
Learning new songs I've never heard
That are far more different to the rest.

Don't forget about science
It's fun but disgusting too.
Doing all sorts of weird experiments
Loads of things to do.

Maths is very important
I really, really like it.
Lots of sums to think about
So it can be hard a bit.

English is brilliant,
Writing stories, poems and more.
Learning about types of grammar too
It's hardly ever a bore.

Now it's nearly the end of the day
We're all so tired by then
Then the bell rings loud and clear
Home time!
And the next day it all happens again.

Emily Cartwright (10)
Brook House Junior School

Sleeping Beauty

In a castle far away
A baby princess there she lay
With fairies all around her now
Granting wishes without knowing how

Then came a fairy, evil enough
Really, she was a bit rough
Then on her eighteenth birthday
She really, really wanted to play

But the evil fairy cast a spell
And then one day she had a fall
She lay in bed for one hundred years
Everyone was crying real tears

And then one day a handsome prince came
Eric was the prince's name
And then he kissed her upon the lips
And then he fell upon her hips

She, awoken by a real surprise
She, sat upright before his eyes
And then they all chuckled with laughter
Time to end happily ever after.

Sarah Simpson (10)
Brook House Junior School

Little Red

There once was a girl with silky blonde hair
And she was sitting in her room on her little wooden chair.
Her mum opened the door and then she said,
'Your granny is ill Little Red.'
Her mum gave her a muffin and some brandy too
She walked downstairs and shouted, 'I've lost a shoe!'
She set out to town and caught a tram
She passed Superdrug and saw a wolf with a pram.
Now this wolf was a bully, a big one too,
Then the tram stopped and she knew what to do.
She got off the tram and she walked straight on
And then when she looked the wolf was gone.
Wolf was already knocking on Granny's door
And when little Granny answered she saw
His great big claws and his perfect paws
I hope he won't eat me, Granny thought
And then she remembered what she had bought.
She ran inside and brought something out
Bang, bang, bang and the wolf was knocked out.
Granny went back in and fell asleep on her bed
But Wolf had got up and soon Grandma was dead!
As quick as he could, Wolf put on her clothes
(He had a fussy taste so he hadn't eaten those!).
He ran and lay down in her comfortable bed
And he waited and waited for Little Red.
Red arrived and said, 'Grandma, may I come in?'
'Just open the door, there's a spare key under the bin.'
Little Red walked in and saw her gran
And this is what she said,
'What big ears you have.'
'All the better to hear you with Hen.'
'What big arms you have.'
'All the better to hug you with Hen.'
'What big teeth you have.'
'All the better to eat you with.'
And the wolf gobbled her up!

Amber Cowan (9)
Brook House Junior School

The Desperate Journey

Packing bags to go to the sea
Going camping, you and me.
Let's have fun, let's have cheer
Don't let Dad get the beer.

Needing toilet on the way
But where on the motorway?
Got to go to that loo
On my gosh, I need a poo!

'Don't you start,' says dear old mum
'I told you this before we come!'
'Please don't nag Mum,' I say
'Especially on the motorway.'

My tank is full of lots of juice
Oh my gosh, my seatbelt's loose.
'It's because of all that pop,'
Says angry Mum in a strop.

Finally we are here
What a change, Dad's had no beer.
But I'm dying for the loo
And I need a drink or two.

I rush and rush to the ladies
It is full of lots of babies.
I see one empty, it is mine,
Once I'm on it I am fine,
Ahhh!

Charlotte Carter (11)
Brook House Junior School

My Family And Me

Dad is like a dog with a great big yawn
Mum is like a lion sprawled on the lawn
My sister's like a cat climbing up the tree.

Olivia Oldfield (8)
Brook House Junior School

Fearful Creation

Tiger, tiger, a fearful creation
A captivating sight
An elegant cunning creature
A vicious feline savage

Your scintillating eyes
Dazzle stars above you
With your magnificent gems
Scanning the forest for your unfortunate prey

Exquisite luminous embers
Swaying through trees
Fierce talons like blades
Shredding the forest floor

Threatening teeth
Attached to a velvet red mouth
Stalking stealthily under the moon
A lonely feline on the prowl

When prey is in sight
Your leap is captivating
Shredding the sinews of an unexpecting heart
Until your vast stomach is full

After your fearful night
You purr constantly
Waiting for unfortunate tomorrow
Tiger, tiger, a fearful creation.

Chloe Davis (10)
Brook House Junior School

Walter The Boxer

There was a young boxer called Walter
He came from the Island of Malta
One day in the ring
He stepped on a spring
And bounced all the way to Gibraltar.

Harry Seaman (10)
Brook House Junior School

Ling Lang Long

(Based on 'The Ning Nang Nong' by Spike Milligan)

On the ling lang long
Where the cats go *pong*
And the dogs go kissy kissy koo
On the lang long ling
Where the fish go *ping*
And the rabbits of bingy bongy boo.

On the ling long lang
Where the tigers go *bang*
And the lions go tingy tangy too.

So it's ling lang long
Cats go *pong*
Lang long ling
Fish go *ping*
Ling long *lang*
Tigers go *bang!*

What a noisy place to be is the ling lang long lang long.

Katherine Leflay (10)
Brook House Junior School

My Baby Cousin Katie May

My baby cousin Katie May
Always fills her nappy
She's sick on her daddy's shoulder
I don't think he's very happy!

Her mummy is my auntie Lisa
Her daddy is my uncle Russ
I always have to calm her down
Because she makes an awful fuss

When it comes to parties
She pulls her brother along
She loves to eat jelly and custard
But she always bites her tongue.

Eleanor Johnson (9)
Brook House Junior School

Goldilocks And The Three Bears

In a forest in a wood
Stood a cottage clean and good.
A perfect cottage comfy and snug
Where Father Bear gulped tea from a mug.
The family were looked after by Mummy Bear
A perfect family very rare.
While Baby Bear was playing games
Mummy bear shouted everyone's names.
'Come, come, let's go for a walk
We can have a little talk.'
Goldilocks came and opened the door
'Ooh, what sweet porridge, I'll have some more.'
Then she wanted to sit down
But she was such a clown
You'll never guess what,
She crushed Baby Bear's chair, (the whole lot!)
Later she went upstairs and got into bed
She fell asleep holding Baby Bear's ted.
The bears came back and they had a big fight
At the end Goldilocks ran home into the night.

Charlotte Ward (9)
Brook House Junior School

Ben The Baby

Ben the baby, ooh what should I say?
Ben the baby likes eating hay!
Ben the baby is a bit fat
That's probably because he ate his sister's cat!

Ben the baby is really deranged
And he once made all the carpets stained.
Ben once beat the brain out of me
That'll show you how naughty he can be.

Ooh I better shut up now, Ben's coming
And I'm running.

Harry Holt (9)
Gilamoor CE Primary School

There's Something In The Wardrobe

There's something in the wardrobe
Comes out every night,
Once I caught a glimpse of it
It gave me quite a fright.

It's got three big eyes
And one tiny nose
And it's obvious to tell
It's got fingers and toes.

It comes from planet Zulu
It's the hairstyle you see,
It's running towards the bathroom
I think it needs a pee!

Now it's coming close
But wait, hang on,
It's got something on it's hair,
Oh no, it's my pom-pom.

What does it want with that?
I need it for later,
Now it's gone back in the wardrobe
It's got a job as a waiter.

Bethany Haughton (11)
Gilamoor CE Primary School

Christmas Night

It is Christmas night
And a man comes down the chimney and gives me a fright.
Dressed in red with big black boots
Putting down the presents and up he shoots.
My sister comes in at 7 o'clock
We go downstairs and there is a shock.
Lots of presents lie under the tree
We are all happy and giggle with glee.

Faye Nicholson (11)
Gilamoor CE Primary School

Why?

Why do I suck my thumb?
Why does it go numb?
Why are cats furry?
Why do they purr?
Why is my cat a pest?
Why do I think she is the best?
Why is my brother crazy?
Why doesn't he have wavy hair?
Why do cats run away and come back?
Why don't they pack?
Why do people think your brain is wrinkly?
Why do people think your brain is pink?
Why did they invent cinemas when you have a television at home?
Why did they invent gnomes?

Bethany Flinton (8)
Gilamoor CE Primary School

Christmas Delight

Tucked in my bed all snugly and warm
Waiting for the early hours of dawn.
My brother Ted did not make a squeak
When he heard the patter of my tiny feet.
As I crept downstairs to take a look
I heard the sound of a heavy foot.
In our living room with a great white beard
Stood Santa Claus looking very weird
With soot on his face and his clothes too
He gave me a smile and went straight up the shoot.
Under the tree was a beautiful sight
Lots of presents which filled the room with delight.

Daisy Robbins (11)
Gilamoor CE Primary School

Spring

I can see sheep giving birth to newborn lambs.
Grass starting to grow again.
Mowers starting to mow the long thin grass again.
I can hear sheep bleating loudly
Tractors roaring their engines as they cut the grass.
I can smell the sheep's wool and the new grass coming up.
I can feel dry grass beneath my feet that is colder than frost.
I can taste Easter eggs melting in my mouth.

Matthew Hellowell (8)
Gilamoor CE Primary School

From A Car Seat

(Inspired by 'From A Railway Carriage' by Robert Louis Stevenson)

Faster than fairies,
Faster than witches,
Bridges zoom over us,
And houses pass by
Hedges and ditches.

And we're charging along like troops in a battle
All through the meadows along they go
Horses and cattle stare at us as we go by.

We're getting closer and closer and there's a mouse crawling up my
back with terrible fear
But the best is, it's getting funnier and funnier as well.
But oh no, a megaton has just happened in the engine
The journey is coming to a close so we're going to our destination and
off we go.

Owen Hayhurst (8)
Gilamoor CE Primary School

Spring

I can see the new flowers in blossom
And newborn lambs chewing on the grass.
As their mothers watch them so no one can catch them
I smell diesel from the tractors as they trudge by our house
leaving muddy tracks on the road.
I can hear the baaing of the lambs and the sheep in the field.
I can feel the hard rocks on the bottom of my shoes
as I walk down the road
I can taste the fresh air sliding down my throat
like the big dipper roller coaster.

Joe Robbins (9)
Gilamoor CE Primary School

The Fairground

I hear the people on the rides
Screaming again and again
Unless they're babies of course
They wouldn't be screeching then.

There are men shouting, 'Go, go, go!'
Others are shrieking, 'No, no, no!'
I can smell the strong smell of lemonade
I see the elderly playing croquet.

My dad's just won the gerbil run
My mum just lost because she slipped in the muck.
I wish I could do all that
They said I'd be good at hook-a-duck!

Billie Cheney (8)
Gilamoor CE Primary School

Dear Auntie Sally

Dear Auntie Sally while you were away . . .
The toilet exploded,
The cat managed to reach the scissors and cut its tail off,
The new carpet, you know the one that cost £100, turned black!
All the plates just jumped into the washing machine one by one
and smashed!
The remote flew from the sofa to the new plasma TV set,
The tap mysteriously overflowed,
The bunk bed split in two because the cat jumped on it
So while you went shopping I went to a sleepover at Lucy's house
for the night.

Leah Preston (10)
Gilamoor CE Primary School

My Birthday

I can see the powerful lights beaming at me.
I can see the people playing everywhere.
I can hear people screaming in my ear very, very, very badly.
I can hear the music playing like mad.
I can smell the sweet delicious cake.
I can smell the sweet party food in my mouth.
I can feel the massive balloons popping in my hand.
I can feel my friends taking my hand and playing with me.
I can taste the lovely cracking cake in my mouth.
I can taste the sweet smell of party food.

Erin Nicholson (7)
Gilamoor CE Primary School

My Name's Bert

My name's Bert
I live in the dirt.
I have a friend
He's round the bend.
I have a dad
He is a bit mad.
I have a mum
She's forever chewing gum.
I have a pet worm
He's called Squirm.
My name's Bert
And I live in the dirt.

Ruaraidh McGill (10)
Gilamoor CE Primary School

Babushka

A twinkling star floating closer and closer
Near to the villagers as slow as a lovely ladybird.
Ecstatic villagers gossiping as loud as thunder
Multicoloured Babushka too busy cleaning.
Strong handsome kings arrived for food
Rest, peace, quiet and to have a little snooze.
Munching, crunching delicious feast, lots of marvellous food.
Sadly the kings waved and set off to find the royal baby.
Beautiful Babushka polished the trusty dusty toys.
She searched and searched from village to village
Beautiful Babushka couldn't give up.

Lena Abdurub (8)
Hucklow Primary School

Bullying

I am the boy who gets bullied.
I am the boy who is petrified.
I am the boy who is in tears and gets injured.
I am the boy who gets lonely.

They are the boys who bully me.
They are the boys who are nasty,
They make fun of me.
They are the boys who make me miserable.
They are the boys who make me unhappy.

Musaid Saleh (8)
Hucklow Primary School

Bonfire Night

Fire is very hot
Fire is exciting
Fire is hot and exploding
Fireworks shining
Fireworks sound like a volcano exploding.

James Lacey (8)
Hucklow Primary School

Baboushka

A beautiful star in the dark sky
People running around the houses
Baboushka cleaning her house
The kings come to stay
The kings gobble up lots of delicious chips.

Patrick Collins (8)
Hucklow Primary School

Snow

Slippery snow soft and white
Steep mountain rocky and misty
Spiky branch hard and stiff
Bushy tree spiky and tall like an arrow shooting to the twinkling star.

Mona Shaibi (7)
Hucklow Primary School

Happiness

It's a beautiful purple princess
That stands beside me holding my hand.
Green eyes sparkling with joy,
Shiny hair glistening in the sun,
Wide mouth always grinning cheerfully,
Glinting body always ready to join the fun,
Warm hands helping and waving,
Sparkling trainers ready to jump and play

I try to keep it with me all the time
Because it's a pleasure,
It tries to get away from me
And it always does succeed.

Jumainah Saiyed (10)
Hyrstmount Junior School

Animals

A dog's saliva is like rain.
A rabbit can jump like a kangaroo.
A caterpillar is green like grass.
A hedgehog's spike is like thorns.
A monkey is as funny as a clown.
A bird flies like an aeroplane.

Saad Daji (9)
Hyrstmount Junior School

Colours

Red is fiery, fiery hot,
Brown is the colour of a lovely pot.
Orange is like the setting sun,
Black and white makes a wonky nun.
Pink is like beautiful love,
White is like a flying dove.
Blue is like a bird flying high,
Green is like a mountain in the sky.
So now you've found out about some colours
So why don't you do all the others.

Mahdiyya Malek (8)
Hyrstmount Junior School

The Writer Of This Poem

(Inspired by 'The Writer of this Poem' by Roger McGough)

Is as chatty as a chatterbox.
Is as sharp as a tent.
Is as noisy as a clown.
Is as funny as a man.
Is as clever as a teacher.
Is as funny as a puppet show.
Is as colourful as a rainbow.

Nabilah Kathrada (7)
Hyrstmount Junior School

Animals

A rabbit is as white as snow,
A caterpillar is as green as grass.
A butterfly is as colourful as a rainbow,
A snake is as slippery as the wet flood.
A bird's legs are as thin as twigs,
A monkey is as fast as the fastest song,
A boy's saliva is as wet as rain.

Aadam Patel (9)
Hyrstmount Junior School

The Angry Sea

The angry sea is as loud as a dinosaur.
The angry sea is crashing on the dirty stones.
The angry sea is light as the sky.
The angry sea is as bubbly as baby shampoo.
The angry sea is as wavy as the roller coaster.
The angry sea is scary and dangerous.

Abdullah Mamaniat (7)
Hyrstmount Junior School

Colours

Red is like fire burning hot,
Yellow is like the colour of a lemon,
Orange is like the resting sun,
Green is like leaves on the trees,
Blue is like the splashing sea,
White is like the floating clouds,
Pink is like true love,
Black is like the shimmering night.

Saudah Chopdat (8)
Hyrstmount Junior School

The Sea

The sea is as strong as rock.
The sea is as loud as a lion's roar.
The sea is as deadly as a sharpened knife.
The sea is as bubbly as a bubble bath.
The sea is as sizzly as a saucepan.
The sea is as terrifying as a tiger.
The sea is like a raging rhino.
The sea is as dark as night.
The sea is as cranky as a gorilla without food.

Mohammed Hashim Ravat (9)
Hyrstmount Junior School

Freedom Is . . .

The lines and squiggles on the page,
The shapes in the orange numeracy book,
The fish swimming in the dark blue ocean,
The healthy green leaves on the tree,
The swirly traffic lights on the page,
The white clouds up in the blue sky,
The green scary crocodile on the page,
The pinky blue plump fish in the dark blue ocean.

Aarifah Seedat (8)
Hyrstmount Junior School

The Angry Sea

The sea was as angry as a man.
The sea was like a man stamping his feet.
The sea was like someone throwing stuff.
The sea was like banging on the stones.
The sea was blue and black and grey.
The sea was like thunder.

Muhammed Laher (9)
Hyrstmount Junior School

Pigeons

Pigeons, pigeons in the sky
Pigeons, pigeons way up high.
Pigeons, pigeons, pigeons, pigeons,
Pigeons, pigeons, very white
Showing up in the night
With the shiny moonlight.

Maryam Chothia (8)
Hyrstmount Junior School

I Am

I am the plump fish swimming in the calm sea.
I am the lines bouncing up and down on the page.
I am the scribbles all over the plain piece of paper.
I am the shiny doors opening and closing.
I am the crocodile snapping its razor-sharp teeth.
I am the snake slithering in the cheerful jungle.
I am the bubbles floating in the blue sky.
I am the fly zooming up in the sky.
So now you know who I am you might like to meet me!

Fatimah Popat (9)
Hyrstmount Junior School

Freedom

The sky is dark blue,
The midnight painter is scary,
The owl is howling,
The birds are screeching out loud,
The floppy white funny-kind-of-looking monster,
I am the scary hairy lion, scaring people away,
I am the blue wavy sea.

Maaria Bahadur (8)
Hyrstmount Junior School

Animals

A dog's eyes are as dark as coal in the fire.
A rabbit is as fluffy as a cloud.
A caterpillar is green like an apple.
A hedgehog is spiky like a horn on the tree.
A monkey swings like a machine.
A bear's legs are like a long stick.

Ebrahim Momoniat (8)
Hyrstmount Junior School

Birds

When I crack open I can do anything I want to do
I can fly anywhere I want to.
My nest is very cosy with my mum and family.
I can make my own nest just how I like it.
I can play and jump wherever I want to.
I can run away wherever I want.
I can shout when I want to.
All my life is about freedom.

Rokeya Karolia (8)
Hyrstmount Junior School

Colours Of The Rainbow

Red is the colour of blood
Orange is the colour of oranges
Yellow is the colours of a banana
Green is the colour of wavy grass
Blue is the colour of the sky
Indigo is the colour of blueberries
Purple is the colour of dark paint.

Maariya Rafiq (8)
Hyrstmount Junior School

Butterflies

Butterflies are symmetrical.
Butterflies are spotty and they are very high in the blue sky.
Butterflies are pretty when they fly.
Butterflies are colourful like a rainbow.
Butterflies have antennas.
Butterflies are free to fly.

Tasneem Badat (8)
Hyrstmount Junior School

Freedom Is . . .

The freezing cold water floating away onto the curvy paths,
The stormy dark clouds surrounding everything down below
                                        in the mystic smoke,
The spooky brown trees anchored into the wet yellow grass swaying
                                        in the breezy wind,
The scary, calm sea flowing onto the rocky damp path,
The tall everlasting hills swaying in the distance,
The freezing cold drops of water falling slowly onto the trees high
                                        above the mountains.

Amina Rawat (11)
Hyrstmount Junior School

Freedom Is . . .

I am stormy clouds in the miserable dull weather,
I am smoke and steam in the misty grey sky,
I am bendy, curvy trees anchored to the soft ground,
I am freezing perishing water,
I am a calm peaceful relaxing lake,
I am mountains as high as the big blue sky,
I am curvy hills in the dark green grass,
I am dark clouds,
I am this spooky monstrous haunted scene,
I am freedom!

Unaysah Daji (11)
Hyrstmount Junior School

Freedom Is . . .

The calm stream glittering in the moonlight,
The blustering wind chasing the fishing boats,
The steep hills standing at a far distance,
The floppy trees anchored in to the deep green mellow grass,
The mud lying on the path waiting to be walked on,
The trees swaying from side to side,
The wooden boats sailing in the narrow river.

Faatimah Patel (10)
Hyrstmount Junior School

The Sea

The sea is crashing,
The waves are splashing.
The sea is strong water,
The sea is wet,
The sea is cold, it tingles my toes.
The shore is bashing,
The pebbles are smashing.
The waves are crashing,
The dogs are barking
The leaves are turning and are wet like me.
The horses are running,
The people are passing while they are running.

Daanyaal Qadeer (7)
Hyrstmount Junior School

Freedom

I am . . .
A slimy green fish swimming in the dark blue sea,
An amethyst shaped as a leaf,
A black spider crawling on top of the trees,
The calm waves splashing,
The soft brown hands,
The black scribbles on the paper,
The funny shapes on flowers,
The raindrops falling on our heads,
The feet looking like they're going to walk.

Sumaiyah Chopdat (9)
Hyrstmount Junior School

A Chimpanzee's Life Is Exciting And Fun

C utting down trees ruins the fun
H anging from trees to and fro
I n the winter we cuddle up warm
M ornings we're off again hunting for food
P apa comes back with a gibbon in his mouth
A nother animal we've lost from the world
N early gone, our life in pieces
Z oo monkeys locked in cages
E very day a tree's cut down
E very day an animal's killed
S lowly, slowly, day by day, our life is ruined, fallen in pieces

L ong ago the rainforest was beautiful
I 'm a chimpanzee wrecked and broken
F rightened! A gunshot strikes out loud
E xhausted by day, dawn, *bang!* I'm gone.

Catherine Bailey (9)
Ingleby Arncliffe Primary School

Rainforests Destroyed

R ainforests destroyed
A nimals kept in cruel captivity
I n the rainforest day and night
N early extinct some animals are
F ortunately some people care
O nly we can help
R ainforests are their homes
E veryone has a right to live
S o we should help them
T rees are cut down
S o sad . . .

D estruction in rainforests all over the world
E very species in danger of extinction
S o we need to act before animals get extinct
T hey're in danger
R uining their homes
O ne tree cut down every day
Y oung and old people with machines
E veryone should feel ashamed
D ying animals, dying . . .

Helen Bailey (9)
Ingleby Arncliffe Primary School

Rainforest

R oads being built
A nimals dying every day
I nsects buzzing
N umber of animals gone down
F ur coats are made
O h so many trees cut down day, by day
R ainforest
E at each other for survival
S torm comes in easily now
T rees have gone, no shelter now.

Granville Cornforth (10)
Ingleby Arncliffe Primary School

Tiger

Sad and alone
Tiger
In the cage
In the zoo

Sad and alone
Tiger's eyes
Looking gloomy

Sad and alone
His ears
Flat
The tiger listens

Sad and alone
His tail hangs down

Sad and alone
Tiger
In the cage
In the zoo.

Eric Hillary (10)
Ingleby Arncliffe Primary School

Jaguars - Haikus

Jaguars are fast
They hunt their prey to get food
I like jaguars.

Jaguars are free
They have black spots everywhere
They are beautiful.

Adam Wren (9)
Ingleby Arncliffe Primary School

Rainforest

Mine is the canopy under the trees
The lumberjack destroying them in the breeze.
Mine are the sad eyes watching the destruction
Mine are the sad eyes watching the corruption.
I see the steel barrel pointing at me
Then I hear a *bang* and no more I can see.

Angus MacColl (10)
Ingleby Arncliffe Primary School

Chimpanzee - Haikus

Climbing up a tree
Reaching for the bananas
Have them for my tea.

I am in a cage
As people watch me suffer
No one cares for me.

All they do is laugh
I need to be returned home
But no one lets me.

Tom Rudd (9)
Ingleby Arncliffe Primary School

Untitled

Waiting in the rainforest
For the men to come.
Waiting for my life to end,
I'm sitting here dumbstruck.

The sound of machines
Drawing nearer and nearer.
I'm truly going to die,
My destiny is now clearer.

Alex Barlow (10)
Ingleby Arncliffe Primary School

A Jaguar's Life

Here is my life set out on a plate
Slowly going due to the people I hate.
This is my life I'm going to tell
Line on line I'm going to say
About that day.
One day the leaves
Started falling from the trees.
My family curiously put their heads
Quietly against the tree bark.
Feeling the vibration on vibration of drilling
Oh that day we knew that something was up.
Panicking on what to do,
You think you are you going to die and fall down, down, never stopping
Down to a place you've never heard of.
Suddenly you stop there frozen in fear
You hear it loud and clear,
Falling, clashing to the ground
Then the people laughing without a sound,
Then the shot of a gun and the last beat of a heart.
Here is my life set out on a plate,
Here is my family lying in fate.
Here is me standing still
Telling my story loud and clear.

Billie Godley (9)
Ingleby Arncliffe Primary School

Chimpanzee

C himpanzee having fun swinging from vine to vine
H appy as can be with my family
I love the rainforest; I never want to go from my home
M y home is made in a tree with leaves for a bed
P utting food in my home
A ah, running, running as fast as I can, tigers are after me for lunch
N o, I want my mum because men are coming and chopping
    down my home
Z oo, no, don't want to go
E ating fruit and veg for every meal
E verything has changed, all my friends are dead, I think I will be next.

Holly Calder (10)
Ingleby Arncliffe Primary School

Life To Death

Life looks like the blue sky
Life tastes like cakes
Life smells like flowers
Life feels like prickly green grass
Life sounds like the peaceful wind
Life lives happily.

Death looks like the black dull sky
Death tastes like mouldy cheese
Death smells like dead flowers
Death feels like sadness
Death sounds like evil
Death lives like a horrible life.

Charlie Holborn
Ings Primary School

Life And Death

Life
Life looks like the sun setting on the sea
Life tastes like bacon sizzling in the pan
Life smells like melted chocolate cake
Life feels like the warm sun beaming on you
Life sounds like birds singing
Life lives around the world.

Death
Death looks like black rats running along the floor
Death tastes like rotten apples
Death smells like bread gone off
Death feels like rotten bodies
Death sounds like a howling wolf
Death lives throughout the world.

Emma Cowell (11)
Ings Primary School

Love And Hate

Love
Love looks like the sun setting in the distance
Love tastes like a sponge cake, really delicious
Love smells like a freshly made pie
Love feels like a hamster all cuddly
Love sounds like your heart is beating
Love lives inside us waiting to burst out.

Hate
Hate looks like mouldy cheese
Hate tastes like wet paper
Hate smells like sweaty armpits
Hate feels like a gunshot through your head
Hate sounds like a sharp gritty voice
Hate lives in our world.

Georgia Mullin-Kipling (11)
Ings Primary School

Love And Hate

Love
Love looks like strawberries and raspberries.
Love tastes like dark chocolate.
Love smells like tulips and roses.
Love feels like growing flowers.
Love sounds like birds whistling in the trees.
Love lives in your heart.

Hate
Hate is like a burning house.
Hate tastes like sprouts.
Hate smells like rotten eggs.
Hate feels like getting burnt.
Hate sounds like houses getting bombed.
Hate lives at the end of the world.

Luke Welford (9)
Ings Primary School

Sadness And Happiness

Sadness
Sadness looks like winter's frost
Sadness tastes like a missing chocolate cake
Sadness smells like rotten weeds
Sadness feels like an empty world
Sadness sounds like summer disappearing
Sadness lives with unhappy faces.

Happiness
Happiness looks like spring has begun
Happiness tastes like melting warm chocolate
Happiness smells like flowers growing
Happiness feels like going on holiday
Happiness sounds like no wind,
Happiness lives forever no matter what.

Chloe Edwards (11)
Ings Primary School

Happiness And Sadness

Happiness
Happiness looks like a flower growing
Happiness tastes like delicious chocolate
Happiness smells like chocolate cake
Happiness feels like a cuddly teddy bear
Happiness sounds like birds in the sky
Happiness lives all around us.

Sadness
Sadness looks like flowers dying
Sadness tastes like mouldy cake
Sadness smells like rotten cheese
Sadness feels like pins going through you
Sadness sounds like a car screeching on the road
Sadness lives all around us.

Chloe Foley (9)
Ings Primary School

War And Peace

War
War looks like a soggy bit of newspaper
War tastes like a slice of mouldy cheese
Warm smells like cloudy black smoke
War sounds like a smashed window
War lives in all of us.

Peace
Peace looks like the sun shining
Peace tastes like a melting chocolate bar
Peace smells like clean washing
Peace feels like fluffy pillows
Peace sounds like people playing in the park
Peace lives in all of us.

Victoria Johnson (10)
Ings Primary School

Happiness And Sadness

Happiness
Happiness looks like the sun
Happiness tastes like sugar plum
Happiness smells like sweet air
Happiness feels like birds tweeting
Happiness sounds like singing
Happiness lives in your heart.

Sadness
Sadness looks like frost
Sadness tastes like dried bread
Sadness smells like a dead body
Sadness feels like tears dropping
Sadness sounds like someone moaning
Sadness lives in your body.

Louella Sumpton (9)
Ings Primary School

War And Peace

War
War looks like bulls charging
War tastes like blood
War smells like drain water
War feels like a headache
War sounds like drums in our head
War lives in our wide open world.

Peace
Peace looks like the calm blue ocean
Peace tastes like a hot tasty Sunday dinner
Peace smells like blue violets
Peace feels like fresh water
Peace sounds like birds singing in the air
Peace lives in our homes, schools and cities.

Kai Weymes (10)
Ings Primary School

Old Age And Youth

Old age
Old age looks like wrinkly raisins
Old age tastes like vinegar and pepper
Old age smells like sweet perfume
Old age feels like you've walked all the way round the world
Old age sounds like a CD when it has been cracked
Old age lives in all of us.

Youth
Youth looks like rainbows in the sky
Youth tastes like melted chocolate
Youth smells like a summer's day round the pool
Youth feels like fresh fruit
Youth sounds like a bird singing in the morning
Youth lives in all of us.

Leonna Foley (10)
Ings Primary School

Cruelty And Kindness

Cruelty
Cruelty looks like a person screaming
Cruelty tastes like eating a flower
Cruelty smells like a rotten old bone
Cruelty feels like a person unloved
Cruelty sounds like a dog whimpering
Cruelty lives in people around us.

Kindness
Kindness looks like a child dancing
Kindness tastes like eating candy
Kindness smells like a pretty flower
Kindness feels like a nice warm hug
Kindness sounds like a child singing
Kindness lives in the world around us.

Tegan Cooper (10)
Ings Primary School

War And Peace

War
War looks like a never-ending black hole
War tastes like a mouldy orange
War feels like a hundred swords stabbing you
War sounds like loud drums
War smells like fire and smoke
War lives everywhere on Earth.

Peace
Peace looks like a field of daisies
Peace tastes like hot chocolate
Peace smells like lavender
Peace feels like a warm summer's day
Peace sounds like a bird singing
Peace lives all around us.

Bradley Williams (9)
Ings Primary School

Greed And Generosity

Greed
Greed looks like mouldy bread
Greed tastes like sweaty toes
Greed smells like a stinky bomb
Greed feels like an ice cube
Greed sounds like a greedy pig
Greed lives inside of people.

Generosity
Generosity looks like melting chocolate
Generosity tastes like sweet candyfloss
Generosity smells like garlic bread
Generosity feels like love in the air
Generosity sounds like birds singing
Generosity lives in you.

Caitlan Taylor (9)
Ings Primary School

War And Peace

War
War looks like falling leaves
War tastes like black smoky clouds
War smells like mouldy eggs
War feels like jumping off a cliff
War sounds like a herd of bulls
War lives all around us.

Peace
Peace looks like children playing
Peace tastes like melting crunchy chocolate
Peace smells like sweet candyfloss
Peace feels like sunshine
Peace sounds like birds singing
Peace lives inside of us.

Georgia Carter (10)
Ings Primary School

Evil And Good

Evil
Evil looks like fiery flames
Evil tastes like rotting cheese
Evil smells like out of date fish
Evil feels like watery slime
Evil sounds like screeching violins
Evil lives in war.

Good
Good looks like a big posy
Good tastes like melting chocolate
Good smells like Sunday dinner
Good feels like newly bought cotton
Good sounds like beautiful singing
Good lives in our hearts.

Charlotte Cook (9)
Ings Primary School

What Am I Like?

When I wake up in the morning
I am like a super computer
All ready for the day ahead.

After a lengthy shower
I am like a rose
All warm and refreshed.

When I arrive at school
I am like a fully charged battery
Ready for use all day.

In Mr Pickering's maths class
I am like a book
Because I am so bored and the questions are too easy.

At the end of the day
I am still like a fully charged battery
At the end of the day.

After a tasty tea and delicious dessert
I am like a couch potato watching TV.

Ashley Fill (11)
Ings Primary School

Leaves

L eftovers of the warm summer before
E very leaf turning from fires of orange and yellow to a dull brown
A ll things are dying down ready for the harsh winter
V ery beautiful sights emit themselves to our eyes
E ven autumn has to die, when it does its
S ombre and the earth falls to the winter coming.

Enya Horton (11)
Ings Primary School

Divorce And Marriage

Divorce
Divorce looks like fire
Divorce tastes like raw fish
Divorce smells like a stained wedding dress
Divorce sounds like a big argument
Divorce feels as hard as a rock
Divorce lives anywhere.

Marriage
Marriage looks like a silver ring
Marriage tastes like a warm Yorkshire pudding
Marriage smells like Febreze carpet spray
Marriage feels like a big hug
Marriage sounds like piano music
Marriage lives in anyone's heart.

Ellie Taylor (9)
Ings Primary School

Love

Love is the colour red.
It tastes like nice melted chocolate.
It smells like fresh roses.
Love looks like a bride on her wedding day.
Love makes me happy, excited as love should be all around us.

Jasmine North (8)
Ings Primary School

Banana

Banana is yellow and swishy
Banana is yummy, that's what I think
Banana is like the daffodils in spring
Banana is like the sun, that's what I think.

Abby Forrester (8)
Ings Primary School

Autumn

This time of year Hindus and Sikhs celebrate Diwali.
This time of year we have Bonfire Night.
This time of year we wear gloves, hats and scarves.
This time of year we raise money for Children in Need.

Gagandeep Manota (8)
Ings Primary School

Autumn

A ll winds changing directions
U nder trees covered in leaves
T ree branches moving with the wind
U nder covers we lie
M oving leaves swarm everywhere
N ight drawing near every night, all dark.

Grant William Marshall (11)
Ings Primary School

Strawberries

Red like blood
Small as a mouse
As juicy as can be
Splat as you step on them!
Strawberries taste sweet
Strawberries!

Leah Robinson (8)
Ings Primary School

Santa's Grotto

Santa's grotto is a wonderful place
Dolls and balls and drums in their case.
Elves a-hammering at a Christmas tree
Green leaves are flying one, two, three!
Icicles are hanging and swinging on my nose
The coldness is going through me, right to my toes.
Just one thing to say, now don't cry a tear
Have a very Merry Christmas and a Happy New Year

Elizabeth Pickering (8)
Ings Primary School

Love

Love is red.
It tastes like tasty chocolate and smells of big flowers.
Love looks like valentine cards.
It sounds of lovely happiness.

Abbie Everett (8)
Ings Primary School

Autumn

It looks like leaves dancing and shuffling
It sounds like flames from the fireworks.
It's like the feeling of the wind blowing.
It tastes like creamy hot soup.
It smells like a fire getting smokier and smokier.

Lauren Gledson (9)
Ings Primary School

Happiness

Happiness is the colour of bright yellow.
It tastes like chocolate mousse.
Happiness is like the smell of chocolate melting.
Happiness looks like a garden filled with beautiful flowers
And the sound of laughing people.
Happiness is fun.

Megan Pleasance (7)
Ings Primary School

Happiness

Happiness is bright pink.
It tastes like hot chocolate and smells o fresh roses.
Happiness looks like a blue waterfall.
It is the sound of beautiful birds singing.
Happiness makes me feel great.

Daisy Fletcher (8)
Ings Primary School

Anger

Anger is dark green.
It tastes like blood.
It smells like steam.
It sounds like plates smashing.
It feels like hot lava from a volcano.
Anger makes me pop!

Marcus Watson (8)
Ings Primary School

Excitement

Excitement is bright pink.
It tastes like warm carrot cake and smells like lovely purple violets.
Excitement looks like magic waterfalls.
Excitement sounds like quiet laughter.
Excitement feels like a ball of snow.

Jasmine Jade Rushworth (8)
Ings Primary School

Love

Love is red.
It tastes like chocolate in a box and smells like flowers in a bunch.
It looks like dogs snuggling together.
It sounds like a heart beating.
It feels like a lovely rabbit.

Ellie Barnett (7)
Ings Primary School

Fear

Fear is grey.
It tastes like freezing chips.
Fear smells of rotten peas.
It looks like a haunted dark school.
Fear sounds like a wicked witch laughing.
It feels like a creepy spider.
Fear is scary.

Cathy Yeung (8)
Ings Primary School

Love

Love is bright red.
It tastes of lovely chocolates and smells of sweet red roses.
Love looks like logs on a fire.
The sound of romantic music.
Love makes you happy!

Terrileigh Johnson (7)
Ings Primary School

Happiness

Happiness is pink.
It tastes like a chocolate bun and juicy sweets.
It smells of flowers and a sweet strawberry.
Happiness looks like Burghley Castle.
It sounds like the sound of loud children.
Happiness makes me crazy.

Amy Carmichael (8)
Ings Primary School

Strawberry

Mmm, strawberry
Lip-licking strawberry
Drooling, dripping strawberry
Lovely red
Squishy
Sweet
Tasty . . .
Splat!
I dropped it!

Grace Stevenson (8)
Ings Primary School

Sense Poem

Love is the colour of red.
Love tastes like soft chocolate.
Love smells like a red box of chocolate.
Love looks like puppies getting warm together.
Love makes me excited.

Ellie-Mae Wakes (8)
Ings Primary School

In My Special Box
(Inspired by 'Magic Box' by Kit Wright)

I will put in the box . . .
The sparkle from a diamond,
The fluff from a cloud,
The twinkle from a star,
A patch of blue sky,
A moonbeam,
A ray of sunshine,
A fairy's wing,
An angel's tear
And the colours of the rainbow.

Bethany Symes (8)
Ings Primary School

Jack Frost - Haiku

Jack Frost is coming
He comes out to play tonight
He comes out right now.

Alfie Porter (9)
Maltby Lilly Hall Junior School

Wintertime Is Great - Haikus

Wintertime is great!
The trees are covered in snow
It's so beautiful.

It is amazing
I love winter, don't you too?
I can see snowflakes.

Jack Frost is here now
We really need to keep warm
And stay in our house.

Lauren Day (9)
Maltby Lilly Hall Junior School

Snow - Haikus

Winter is here now
Spring, summer, autumn to go
Come everyone, play!

Raindrops on my head
This rain will turn to snow soon
It's snowing outside

All the leaves are off
The trees are bare, let's do stuff
All right then let's play.

Ben Cliff (8)
Maltby Lilly Hall Junior School

Winter Is Very Cold - Haiku

Snowmen are in field
Snowmen, very fun to make
I like winter lots.

Jake Bunting (9)
Maltby Lilly Hall Junior School

Keeping Warm In Winter- Haikus

Stay in the house now
And keep warm with some cocoa
The fire should be on.

Finish your cocoa
Get a hot-water bottle
And keep yourself warm.

When you go to bed
Have something warm next to you,
And you will sleep good.

Francesca Riley (9)
Maltby Lilly Hall Junior School

Winter Is Here – Haikus

Winter is here now
All the leaves have left the trees
Snow is falling now.

Mark Higham (9)
Maltby Lilly Hall Junior School

I Am Snowboarding - Haiku

I am snowboarding
Down a very big, big hill
With my friend Dylan.

Ben Ferguson (9)
Maltby Lilly Hall Junior School

Dark Nights - Haiku

Dark nights are scary
For everyone in the world
It is cold as well.

Aidan Hazell (9)
Maltby Lilly Hall Junior School

Winter - Haikus

Winter is here now
Look at my scarf, it's stripy
My hands are too warm.

Come on play today
We can go sledging with you
We've got loads of snow.

I can feel the rain
I can hear robins singing
The rain is coming.

The sun is coming
The snow is melting today
Goodbye snow, bye-bye.

Shannon Long (9)
Maltby Lilly Hall Junior School

Robin - Haiku

Robin flap your wings
Robin you are beautiful
Robin come to me.

Natasha Connell (8)
Maltby Lilly Hall Junior School

Snow Is Cold And Wet - Haiku

Snow is cold and wet
You can go and build snowmen
Robins on bare trees.

Jack Davies (9)
Maltby Lilly Hall Junior School

Cold Ice Is Slippy - Haikus

Cold ice is slippy
Cars start to slide everywhere
Ice freezes the pond.

Jack Frost comes around
And he freezes all the town
Likes everything cold.

Robins start to fly
Snow starts to fall everywhere
And school starts to end.

Winter trees are bare
Blossom stops to fall today
Snow might fall today.

All ponds start to freeze
And people start to ice skate
We all celebrate.

Jack Belcher (9)
Maltby Lilly Hall Junior School

Cocoa - Haiku

Hot cocoa is warm
It's lovely to have cocoa
I'll get my coat on.

Bradley Callum Marshall (8)
Maltby Lilly Hall Junior School

Winter Is Here - Haiku

Lots of snow is here
They fall down to the hard ground
We can make snowmen.

Jordan Wright (8)
Maltby Lilly Hall Junior School

The Bird In The Tree - Haikus

The bird in the tree
Gently flaps his gorgeous wings
Ready to take flight.

The wind blows strongly
He gives a little jump up
Fluttering his wings.

Lucy Tune (9)
Maltby Lilly Hall Junior School

Cold Nights Coming - Haiku

Cold nights are coming
Everyone snuggled in bed
Before Jack Frost comes.

Rachel Kittle
Maltby Lilly Hall Junior School

Frozen Pond - Haiku

The frozen ice pond
So smooth in the cold winter
The very nice pond.

Libby Barlow (8)
Maltby Lilly Hall Junior School

Jack Frost - Haiku

Jack Frost is coming
He is coming out to play
He is very cold.

Megan Williams (8)
Maltby Lilly Hall Junior School

Winter Is Ice-Cold - Haikus

Winter is ice-cold
With a frosty morning scene
The trees are bare now.

Declan Hewitt (8)
Maltby Lilly Hall Junior School

Tiger

Stalking his prey
Darting round trees at the speed of light
Glaring eyes staring everywhere
Sharp claw marks on every tree
Pointed teeth glistening in the moonlight.

Jonathan Parr (10)
North & South Cowton Primary School

Parrots

Parrots of all colours
Red, yellow and blue
Lots of different kinds
Gliding like a plane
Coming in to land
Many shapes and sizes
My favourite the scarlet macaw
Puffing up in the cold
Feathers as red as a burning fire.

Jack Walmsley (8)
North & South Cowton Primary School

Polar Bears

Polar bear, long gleaming white fur keeping it warm
in the cold winter's air.
Young like small fluffy clouds, bouncing around, having fun
on the frozen ice.
So strong that they can crush anything in their path.
Quick paws catching fish by the shoal,
Smashing the snow with their heavy body to catch underground prey,
Travelling for miles searching for places to live.

James Armstrong (10)
North & South Cowton Primary School

Horse Noise

As the horse gallops around
This lovely beating sound makes me so proud.
As the horse gets a drink with a splashing noise
And then says, 'Thank you,' with neigh.
Time for bed, get in the hay
With a loud snore.
See you in the morning and we can gallop some more.

Maisie Imogen Price (10)
North & South Cowton Primary School

Dogs

I love all dogs whatever they are.
I don't care what shape or colour they are.
All the different breeds of dogs
But my favourite dogs are the boxers and greyhounds,
Dalmatian and guard dogs.
I love all dogs whatever they are.

Thomas James Lockwood (9)
North & South Cowton Primary School

Cheetah

Cheetah, racing swiftly,
Stalking its prey,
Fur sticking up like a sharp thorn.
Hunting in the day,
Males sleeping, females pouncing.
African sun,
Killing wildebeest,
Along with gazelle
With sharp claws and razor-sharp teeth.

Carl Hughes (9)
North & South Cowton Primary School

Doggy Haiku

Doggies are funny
Though they may chew your homework
But they are still cute.

Leah Smith (9)
Oakhill Primary School

Thin Caitlin, Fat Dan!

There once was a girl called Caitlin
Who was as thin as a stick or a pin.
Her brother called Dan,
Loved Coke in a can
Which made him the size of a bin.

Caitlin Franklin (8)
Oakhill Primary School

The Girl Called Mathilda

There once was a girl called Mathilda
Who killed a big fat builder.
She threw bricks at his head
Until he was dead
Then the whole city tried to kill her.

Mathilda Bassnett (8)
Oakhill Primary School

Marks Shark

There was a man called Mark
Who had a tiny pet shark.
He woke in the night,
With a terrible fright
And found out that it could bark.

Joshua Massey (9)
Oakhill Primary School

Young Man

There was a young man with a vest
And he wore it on his chest.
Then his old gran,
Bought him a big van
And he lived in the Wild West.

Tom Sanders (8)
Oakhill Primary School

Seasons - Haiku

Summer in the pool
In winter I go skiing
Spring, collecting leaves.

Jessica Fox (9)
Oakhill Primary School

The Grass Is Green

The grass is green, the sky is blue
Everybody's out except for you.
The clouds are white
But you're alright,
Some are grey
But you can stay.

Jack Lawton (9)
Oakhill Primary School

That Dog Sandy

I have a dog called Sandy
He had a big Uncle Andy.
He lived in a shop
And he likes it when bubbles pop
That silly dog called Sandy.

Thomas Speed (9)
Oakhill Primary School

There Was a Girl Called Jess

There was a girl called Jess
She wore a beautiful dress.
She went to the ball
And had a great fall
And the dress was a terrible mess.

Jessica Wright (8)
Oakhill Primary School

Friendship Poem

If I could catch a star
I would do it just for you
And share with you its beauty
On the day you're feeling blue.

If I could build a mountain
You could call your very own
A place to calm down
And a place to be alone.

If I could take your troubles
I would toss them far away
But all these things
Are impossible for me.

I cannot build a mountain
Or catch a star fair
But let me be what I know best
A friend who's always there.

Leah Harston (9)
Oakhill Primary School

That Very Old Man Called Gill

Once there was a man called Gill
Who had to take a pill.
He took it with water
Just as he ought to
That very old man called Gill.

Christopher David Holling (9)
Oakhill Primary School

Winter

W oolly jumpers are worn as the strong wind is blowing
    against the tall trees
I cicles are falling quickly on the thick snow like a dagger
    being thrown at a soft sponge
N oisy rain is falling on the white snow as the families are gathering
    around their warm fires
T he children are sliding on their sledges like some water
    running down a scope
E ach and every branch outside is covered with thick snow
    like the chocolate on a biscuit
R oads are covered with melting snow as the sun is slowly rising.

Ruairi Lowe (8)
Our Lady of Sorrows Catholic Primary School

Phrase Poem

Chunky, wrinkly, colossal tree falling frighteningly like a rock falling
                                     from a big hill.
Wet, cold, pointy icicle melting slowly like a cold ice cream melting
                                     down the cone.
Circular, white, pointed snowflake falling fast like leaves swirling
                                     from the sky.
Straight, round, sharp post standing still like a tree with no twigs.
Wet, flat, round puddle lying freely like a hot tub flat and calm.

Jack Reeve (9)
Our Lady of Sorrows Catholic Primary School

Winter

W et small ball like a snowball swishing past me fast
 I cy wet shape hanging like a dagger falling on top
    of someone's head
N oisy nippy birds twitter getting twigs ready for winter
T he chunky fat tricky tree swishing from side to side with the wind
    pushing against the tree
E xtra wind pushing slowly like it's going to lift you up to the sky
R ushing snow quickly slowing past your feet like it has got you
    and it is never going to let go.

Mitchell Monaghan (8)
Our Lady of Sorrows Catholic Primary School

Phrase Poem

Dedicated to my Grandad

Colossal, leafless, bare tree waving lively
Like a field of corn calmly swaying in the breeze.
Shimmering, pointy, dripping icicle glowing beautifully
Like a shimmering amethyst glittering in the air.
Cold, white, melting snowflake falling slowly
Like a cold ice cream melting from ice to water.
Rough, hard, gigantic post standing sadly
Like the bark of a tree.
Wet freezing round puddle lying calmly
Like a little lamb sitting in its pen.

Jessica Hassall (9)
Our Lady of Sorrows Catholic Primary School

Winter

W indy, white, frosty wind blowing powerfully like a windmill spinning
 in a tornado

I gloo small and damp freezing cold like an iceberg coming to shore

N arrow, nippy, noisy icicle powerfully dropping like hailstone falling
 from the sky

T wisting thick tree huge and thin like a man guarding
 the queen's house

E verest wet and slippy, freezing cold

R oar sludgy and deep like a plunge of Mount Rushmore.

Oliver Newbert (10)
Our Lady of Sorrows Catholic Primary School

Phrase Poem

Wrinkly, colossal, chunky tree swaying calmly
Like a bunch of flowers gently moving in the breeze.
Thin, cold, smooth icicle shining glamorously
Like a bright, shimmery diamond glittering in the air.
Soft, cold, white snowflake dripping slowly
Like an ice cream just melting to the floor.
Tall, thin, grey post standing still
Like a cat paying no attention and not making or causing any trouble.
Curvy, brown, dirty puddle shrieking sadly like a kitten who lost its
mum.

Amy Fudge (8)
Our Lady of Sorrows Catholic Primary School

Phrase Poem

Leafless, chunky, bare tree falling fast like a motorbike in drift races.
Sparkling, pointing, dripping icicle hanging bravely like a monkey
hanging off a tree with his tail.
Small cold soft snowflake falling gently like a piece of paper slowly
falling from a table.
Tall, metallic, hard post standing still like a soldier guarding
the queen's house.
Wet, shallow, soft puddle drying quickly like a fireman putting out
a house fire.

Joseph Pinkney (9)
Our Lady of Sorrows Catholic Primary School

Winter

W et, dripping, watery icicle frozen solid sitting on the corner of a
house like a dagger waiting to strike
I cy cold puddle sitting in the middle of a road being run through
by a car like a leopard pouncing the fields with the grass brushing
against its fur
N ovember is in winter and nippy icicles are appearing slowly
on the corners of people's houses glistening in the dim
light outside
T rees are twisted, rushing straight down to the ground
E very snowball, swishy and soft falling from the sky immediately
Like an eagle swooping down from the icy windy freezing air.
R unning water rushing rapidly on everybody
turning into freezing cold icicles hanging everywhere.

Ciara Batty (8)
Our Lady of Sorrows Catholic Primary School

Winter

W atery icicle dripping fast like a shower with water blasting out.
I n winter I do ice skating and I whiz like an aeroplane in the sky
N umb fingers turning red like a windmill spinning fast
T rees blowing fast from side to side like a kite flying
   in the strong wind
E very winter we go on the sledge and it whizzes fast like a car
   whizzing down the street
R ushing snow falling down like a rainstorm whooshing from the sky.

Emily Kirkbride (9)
Our Lady of Sorrows Catholic Primary School

Winter

W here the snow falls in a field
I cicles hang off a house waiting to drop somewhere south
N ear a frozen lake, cracking towards a bunch of
T rees with no leaves and buds trying to grow
E ffortlessly in the snowstorm
R eaching for the summer sun.

Aaron Hartin (10)
Our Lady of Sorrows Catholic Primary School

Phrase Poem

Wrinkly, leafless, chunky tree swaying gently
Like a field of moving grass.
Freezing, pointed, wet icicle dripping quickly
Like a sharp needle falling.
Dripping, cold, frozen snowflake falling slowly
Like a gust of whistling wind.
Thin, tall red post standing still like a soldier at attention.
Small, wonky, frozen puddle sitting flat
Like a river frozen over in winter.

Emma Hinchliffe (8)
Our Lady of Sorrows Catholic Primary School

If I Could Travel Back In Time

If I could travel back in time
I'd behead Henry the Eighth,
I'd see what it was like to be a Victorian maid,
I'd ask Florence Nightingale what she wanted most,
I'd ask the Tudors why they dyed their hair with rhubarb,
I'd tell Queen Victoria to stop children working in dangerous places.

Lydia Coote (8)
Rosedale Abbey Primary School

Champp

C hamp is my best horse
H e's very bouncy in canter
A pples are his favourite food
M ane as soft as a cushion
P lays every day with freedom in the fields.

Chloe Marley (8)
Rosedale Abbey Primary School

Hector

H ector eats a lot
E mpty bowl he leaves
C uddly furry rabbit
T aking carrots in his cage
O ff he hurries
R unning he goes.

Bethany Richardson (8)
Rosedale Abbey Primary School

If I Could Travel Back In Time

I would feel the sand of ancient Egypt,
I'd wear Queen Victoria's jewellery,
I'd sail the seas with the Vikings,
I'd explore with Florence Nightingale
And chop off Henry the Eighth's head.

Cara Blackburne-Brace (8)
Rosedale Abbey Primary School

My Ideal Day

Monday I will wake up and eat a sausage sandwich
Then I get post and find I have one million smackers!
My mum says, 'You go look up in your room'
Oh my bedroom is a mountain full of presents!
I have tickets to swim with real dolphins,
A car, a laptop, a magic juice maker,
It must all be a dream
And it is all for me!

Maddie Kenderdine (10)
Rosedale Abbey Primary School

Sooty

S ooty is my best friend
O ver the wall he goes
O n his way to play
T ag he plays with me
Y ou're for it! He runs away.

Liam Thompson (7)
Rosedale Abbey Primary School

If I Could Travel Back In Time

I would travel back to the Victorian age,
I'd wear one of their finest gowns,
I would travel with Florence Nightingale to explore more of her town,
I'd meet Queen Victoria and look around her home
Then I would go to the mining times and see who slept in my room,
Then I would go down to the kitchen and taste all their food.

Olivia Doughty (9)
Rosedale Abbey Primary School

My Ideal Day

I wake up in bed and I find
A bacon sandwich ready to eat,
One hundred pounds off the street.
A hole in my wall shooting out presents,
My brother walks in with two dead pheasants!
I look out the window and see a new car
It is as shiny as a river and as red as rubies.
I wriggle out of bed and open the door
My sister is waiting to give me a manicure.

Annabelle Horseman (11)
Rosedale Abbey Primary School

Tipsy

T ip on the end of his tail
I   get annoyed with him sometimes
P ouncing on walls
S ooty and Tipsy fight
Y awning all day.

Bethany Thompson (7)
Rosedale Abbey Primary School

My Ideal Day

Wake up on a Saturday at 6.30am
To find a continental breakfast right beside me.
I finish it off, every last scrap and look up, wow, there's a genie.
It's blue like a dolphin and eating cherry pie,
He grants me five wishes a day until I die.

Receive a parcel in the post,
Rip it open, it's an easel and paper.
Whatever I draw on, it become reality,
Draw myself a retriever puppy
And lots of money.

Take the puppy for a walk in the park
And suddenly it starts to bark....
It takes me to the climbing frame
Where I find three tickets
To a rock festival
That play any bands I choose.

Wish for my older brother to still be alive
And for my grandad to live next door
And like all the stuff I do.
Get VIP passes to Leeds Superbowl and Flamingo Land
And then KFC for tea!

Thomas Middleton (11)
Rosedale Abbey Primary School

A Strawberry On Your Birthday

This strawberry looks like tomato ketchup oozing out of a burger.
This strawberry screams like a toddler who's cut his knee.
This strawberry feels like a clammy scaly snake.
This strawberry smells like disgusting flaky fish food.
This strawberry tastes like prawns dipped in a dipping sauce.

Alice Gilman (8)
St Olaves School, York

The Winter Man

He sprints across the country
And rockets across the sea
Making everything in sight
As white as white could be.

He makes my feet freeze
And makes me feel numb
From my ankles to my knees.

As he flies past quickly and silently,
All the leaves fall down in pain
For he hurts them with his icy breath.

This cruel bitter man
Makes things cold and glisten
From trees to compost.
You may know his name,
You may not.
He is the one and only
Terrible Jack Frost.

Polly Moss (9)
St Olaves School, York

An Orange On Your Birthday

This orange looks like a decaying skull.
This orange screams like a banshee when it is peeled.
This orange feels like a slimy slug.
This orange smells like a rotten frog.
This orange tastes like a disgusting mushroom.

Natasha Bell (9)
St Olaves School, York

The Squire

Once in the poor town of Doncaster,
Where the knights had never heard of Italian pasta.
A young lad was riding his ol' horse,
Though it often strayed from its course.
The young squire,
Was to aspire,
A knight by sixteen,
Yes, he was keen.
Two years of hard training,
Through droughts and through raining,
His master, Sir Richard,
Was kind but worked him hard.
On the squire's sixteenth birthday,
Squire heard him say,
'A fine lad,
Just like his dad.
On his birthday,
If he passes his test,
He'll be named O' Sir Tempest,
The best present,
Followed by a feast of the finest pheasant.'
Squire dashed in
And desperately thanked him.
Little did he know
It was the final time he'd do so.
Richard gave him a smile
As they rode a mile
To the arena,
Where a man he would beat a.
Richard wished him good luck,
While out stepped the crook.
He gasped in surprise
As out stepped Jonny-no-Ties.
He was set to fight
Under serious fright.
He was to slay a giant of man
Who could snap a frying pan.
They were ready, up they got,
Fear and happiness all forgot.

The horses were off,
(They'd done with the trough)
Lances were out,
Squire gave Jonny a clout,
Jonny was unfazzled,
Though the crowd was dazzled.
Jonny sighed and swung,
So Squire fell in dung.
The swords were drawn,
They parried across the lawn.
The crowd cheered,
Whilst the horses reared,
Squire fell down,
Jonny smiled like a clown.
Well, the young squire
Used to aspire,
A knight by sixteen,
Yes, he was keen.
Two years of hard training,
Through droughts and through raining,
Not long enough.
Oh well, he fought tough,
But Jonny-no-Ties
Out of squire was made pies.
So that was the end of the squire.

Emma Thompson (11)
Serlby Park School

The World

The world, it's such a scary place,
The world it goes at a certain pace.
Africa, France, Australia too,
A little pig in a talent show dancing in a pink tutu!
The world is such a surprising place,
The world, it's like a big shoelace.
A puzzle is the world.
Can we ever work out a solution?

Gemma Rodger (9)
Serlby Park School

My Family

My nanna, my nanna is a cooking queen,
She's the best at scones, also beans.

My brother, my brother, the clumsy clutter
And also a nutter.

My grandad, my grandad is a very good painter
And also gives my brother fruit.

My mum, my mum is always telling me to do my chores,
So I just say *no*.

My cousin, my cousin is an absolute nutter
And is always forever eating butter.

My dad, my dad is always on the phone,
It bugs my mum when he gets home.

Morgan Kane (9)
Serlby Park School

Horses

Horses, I love the horses on the courses,
Black, gold, silver birch,
Future, past and present,
Most of all I love the real winners,
Kings of the courses,
And that is why I love horses.

Katy Halbert (10)
Serlby Park School

My Uncle

My uncle is a copper,
My uncle is a rocker,
My uncle really likes his soccer,
He's always cleaning his brass knocker,
And that's my uncle.

Shannon Smith (11)
Serlby Park School

Serlby Park

S inging and laughing in the playground
E ntertaining all around
R unning in football, *yes I scored!*
L unchtime is coming
B ell's ringing, maths is over
Y elling in the playground, whistle is blowing

P utting our coats on a peg
A fter that we get changed for PE
R aining outside, it's a miserable day
K eep our coats on, we're on our way.

Thomas Michael Maule (9)
Serlby Park School

I Like

I like football,
I like cricket,
I like golf,
I like fishing,
I like cooking,
But most of all
I like being me.

Callum Rudd (11)
Serlby Park School

Water, Water

Water, water everywhere,
Always dropping from the air,
Making puddles on the ground,
Flash floods destroying the town,
Panic, panic, running away,
Wishing this could go away.

Benjamin Oxley (10)
Serlby Park School

Seasons

Spring showers,
Not many flowers,
Leaves budding on the trees,
Soon there will be many buzzy bees.

Summer season is the best,
Kids running round in shorts and vest,
Barbecues, parties, pools and fun,
And the school holidays have just begun.

Autumn brings us Hallowe'en,
Lots of scary monsters to be seen,
Also brings us Bonfire Night,
Bangs and crashes, fires burning bright.

Winter chills all around,
Sparkly frost on the ground,
Father Christmas is soon to appear,
Christmas Day is almost here.

Jade Lyons (10)
Serlby Park School

Fear Poem

Fear is black like a dark stormy night.
It tastes like mouldy old rotting milk.
It smells like smoke from your bonfire.
It looks like an old trash can with flies flying around.
It sounds like people screaming as loud as they can.
It feels like being on a dark lonely street on your own.

Ben Bishop (9)
Sitwell Junior School

I'm Trying To Save The Environment

I'm through with driving my 4x4,
It's a gas guzzler
So I've bought a Toyota with unleaded fuel.
I'm trying to save the environment,
It's starting to work,
But I need you to stop polluting in your petrol cars.

I'm through with fossil fuel
It's going to run out.
So I've bought solar panels for my house.
I'm trying to save the environment,
It's starting to work,
But I need you to stop wasting the world's resources.

I'm through with deforestation
It's a needless thing,
So I've started recycling papers and magazines.
I'm trying to save the environment,
It's starting to work,
But you need to start recycling too.

I'm through with destroying the ozone layer,
It's our fault,
So I wrote this poem.
I'm trying to save the environment,
It's starting to work,
But you need to help too.

Edward Spink (10)
Sitwell Junior School

Cloud

C louds are white and fluffy in the sky
L ovely clouds are wandering round
O h I wish I could walk on them
U nder the blue sky
D reaming of the fairy land.

Mariam Hussain (8)
Sitwell Junior School

Chocolate

C runchy, hard dark chocolate
H eavenly chocolate melting in my mouth
O n top of the chocolate was caramel running down my chin
C ream around the edge of it
O ooh, so chocolatey
L ovely, lovely chocolate
A n extraordinary chocolate cone
T offee in the middle
E veryone wanting to taste it.

Alexandra Marrison (8)
Sitwell Junior School

At Night

At night the moon shines bright
Over the land and sea.
Owls hoot and whistle
Far above in the trees.
At night it is like
The trees are singing to me,
'Close your eyes and drift off to sleep.'
So I do Zzzzzzz.

Rachael Hill (9)
Sitwell Junior School

White Fluffy Snow

White fluffy snow falling to the ground,
Quietly, quietly, it makes no sound.
Children play, having fun,
But sadly, sadly here comes the sun.
Slowly, slowly it starts to melt,
Sad, sad, the children felt.

Isobel Hancock (8)
Sitwell Junior School

Polar Poem

Meet the polar bears, they are crying,
Thanks to CO_2 they are frying.
We are destroying their climate of ice
And for the huge fluffy species it's not very nice.
Polar bears, polar bears trudging along the ice
But soon it may be rocks or rubble.
There's no snow but rivers flow.
Why let these wonderful creatures go to waste
At the hands of the human race!

Lewis Waters (11)
Sitwell Junior School

The Falling Frost

The frost is falling down from the sky,
It twists and turns from way up high.
It falls from the trees and lands on the floor
And then it comes down more and more.
Then the sun comes out again
And the grass goes all plain.

Georgia Barnard (9)
Sitwell Junior School

A Winter's Day In England

The grass is very frosty,
The clouds are like a bucket of frost,
Trees are coated in white icing,
Jack Frost has been busy
Painting windows glimmering silver.
The fog is a grey cover,
Hiding everything from sight.

Kyle Allen (8)
Sitwell Junior School

Deforestation, Depression

Burning wood,
Pitch-black mud,
The unfresh smell,
Unhappy sights.

Abandoned trees,
Crackling leaves,
No world, no life,
No atmosphere.

Unpleasant sights,
Swaying trees
Falling down,
Landing on the gruesome ground.

Upon a time
They would stand high.
The proud sights I would see
But now they turn dull and black,
That's not what I'd like them to be.

Leanne Davis (11)
Sitwell Junior School

The Environment

The environment's in danger
And there is little we can do.
All the things that have happened
Are because of me and you.

The fuels are being burned
And are mixing with the air,
Damaging the ozone layer,
Letting the sun's rays through.

Nuclear plants are letting out smoke
And deadly poisonous gases,
Floating up into the sky,
Darkening the world.

Gary Foster (11)
Sitwell Junior School

The Whale, The Whale

The whale, the whale
How could it be
That they are no longer in the sea?
They may be big but inside they are small,
If we carry on we will kill them all.

The whale, the whale
How could it be
The beautiful creature that lives in the sea
Can no longer be viewed by you and me?

The whale, the whale
How could this be?
The people responsible are you and me.

Jennifer Howsego (10)
Sitwell Junior School

Pollution Is A Dragon

Pollution is a dragon,
Pollution is a dragon.

It poisons our air.
Does anyone care?

It kills our fish,
If you care!

It melts our ice caps.
We should despair!

It makes everything bad.
We should be sad!

It makes our water turn to grey.

How do we stop him?
Is there a right way?

Does anybody care?

William Morgan (11)
Sitwell Junior School

The North Pole

Human activities have never helped,
Causing the ice caps to melt.
Snow is glorious when it comes,
It is like a fluffy white blanket.
The North Pole is icy, the North Pole is exquisite.

Human activities have never helped,
Causing the ice caps to melt.
Transport like cars are polluting the air,
Oil is spilling from factory to sea.
The North Pole is dying, the world is guilty.

Human activities have never helped,
Causing the ice caps to melt.
The polar bears are going
'Cause the world stops snowing.
Pollution has never helped.

William Bladon (10)
Sitwell Junior School

Save The Turtles

The turtle, the turtle
Swimming in the sea
Chasing the waves all day.
The turtle, the turtle
With her paddling feet
She splashes to catch her prey.

The turtle, the turtle
Dying in the sand
The people stole her shell.
The turtle, the turtle
Dying in the sand
They took her babies as well
Save the turtles!

Ellie Hancock & Pippa Humphries (10)
Sitwell Junior School

A Winter's Day In England

The frosty grass looks like freezing icicles.
The fog hangs in the air like a blanket of white.
The usually green grass is coated with icing sugar that you put
on a cake.
You can barely see a thing through the white blanket of fog.
Jack Frost has frozen the air, so beware.

Georgia O'Brien (8)
Sitwell Junior School

A Winter's Day In England

The frosty grass is like pieces of ice cream.
It's like the tree is growing white bright hair.

Jack Frost has been scattering his magical,
White powder everywhere.

Freezing fog hangs in the air,
When you walk into it you will disappear.

Lewis Gee (8)
Sitwell Junior School

A Winter's Day In England

Cold winter frost falls to the ground
But when you touch it it will melt.
I know it is a shame
But it will come back again.

When frost appears it covers all the houses.
I guess that Jack Frost did this.
Everything sparkles and glitters like diamonds.

April Ogden (7)
Sitwell Junior School

A Winter's Day In England

No blue sky.
No sun.
No houses.
No cars.
Everything has disappeared
Behind a white blanket of fog.
You can see nothing,
Just thick white fog.
Jack Frost comes every winter
Sprinkling glitter everywhere.

Matthew Brookes (8)
Sitwell Junior School

A Winter's Day In England

Frozen, frosty ice,
It's like a gentle dusting of flour.

I can't see or hear any cars
The fog is so thick.

Every tree is gleaming white with icicles.
Jack Frost arrives in the night,
The icicles look a lovely sight!
Pretty patterns to everyone's delight.

Natty McKenzie-Smith (8)
Sitwell Junior School

Love Poem

Love is white like fluffy white clouds.
Love tastes like warm sweetcorn.
Love smells like Mum.
Love looks like a magic world.
Love sounds like sweet music.
Love feels like a gentle touch.

Amelia Davis (8)
Sitwell Junior School

A Winter's Day In England

The sky was as foggy as a white blanket.
It was as cold as the Atlantic sea.
It was like a diamond shimmering on the ground.
The ice made the grass look like a white icicle.
The ice was whiter than a fluffy white cloud.
The cobwebs had been painted with ice
And were hanging from my window.
The icicles were sharper than sharks' teeth.
Jack Frost came down to my house last night,
He painted my window pale white.

Abbie Ollivant (8)
Sitwell Junior School

A Poem About Feelings

I'm as happy as a monkey with a soft chewy banana.
I'm as happy as a monkey in a forest.
I'm as lonely as a guinea pig in a smelly, damp cage.
I'm as sad as a dog without its large juicy bone.
I'm as unhappy as a cat that's lost its mother.
I'm as happy as a fish with its mother.
I'm as sad as a tiger without its red juicy meat.

Charlotte Hunter (7)
Sitwell Junior School

Fear

Fear is red like thick soup.
It tastes like damp smelly socks.
It smells like mouldy cheese.
It looks like a dark empty house.
It sounds like big footsteps coming towards me.
Fear feels like I am alone.

Michael Rose (9)
Sitwell Junior School

A Poem About Feelings

I'm as happy as a monkey with a soft chewy banana.
I'm as happy as a monkey in a green tall forest.
I'm as lonely as a guinea pig in a smelly cage.
I'm as sad as a dog without its nice juicy bone.
I'm as unhappy as a cat that's lost its mum.
I'm as happy as a dog running in the park.
I'm as sad as a monkey without his soft banana.
I'm as lonely as a guinea pig stuck in his boring cage.

Thomas Woolley (8)
Sitwell Junior School

Love Poem

Love is red like soft delicate roses.
Love tastes like sweet creamy ice cream melting in your mouth.
Love smells like fresh, beautiful, new flowers.
Love looks like a newborn baby.
Love sounds like birds tweeting softly.
Love feels like warm loving hugs.

Kay Russell (9)
Sitwell Junior School

Happiness Poem

Happiness is yellow, like the burning sun.
It tastes like sweet juicy tomatoes.
It smells like lovely smelling cake.
It looks like a street full of comfort.
It sounds like a lonely breeze rushing past me.
It feels like nice soft fur.

Matthew Bailey (9)
Sitwell Junior School

The Olympic Games

Welcome to the Olympic Games,
London, the year twenty-twelve.
In everyone there is a winner,
But you have to dig and delve.

Starting with the sprinter,
The one with endless grace,
He is a speeding bullet,
With a red, sweaty face.

Second there is a wrestler,
A tower of stone,
And at the end of each match,
His opposition starts to moan.

The third event is by far the best,
A leaping grasshopper,
Flying over the sand with ease,
A brilliant long jumper.

Fourth is an elastic wonder,
Turning in mid air,
She is such a good gymnast,
Others can't help but stare.

Last there is a flow of energy,
Blink and you'll miss her,
She is extremely fast,
An excellent swimmer.

Now the games are over,
England got all gold,
That's a tale to tell the grandkids,
When we get really old.

Maddie Shellcock (10)
Sitwell Junior School

Knuckle Walker

It's a . . .
    Silver back
    Ready for attack
    Chest pounder
    Tree lounger
    Banana muncher
    Ground puncher
    Bone cruncher
    Back huncher
    Plant hooker
    Danger ducker
    Big challenger
    It's here to scare
    Fearless predator
    Big black teddy bear.

George Bean & Matthew Aistrop (10)
Sutton Park Primary School

Fibonacci

Problem solver
Code cracker
Golden lover
Shape liker
Hindu follower
Snail observer
Brain worker
African liver
Dead forever.

Tom Marton (10)
Tickton CE Primary School, Beverley

Without Words

If all the words were spoken, used up, ran out,
We wouldn't be able to write our names,
We wouldn't be able to count to 10 in numbers,
We wouldn't be able to say please or thank you,
We wouldn't be able to choose our favourite sweets,
We wouldn't be able to learn,
We wouldn't be able to talk to other people,
We wouldn't be able to socialise with different people,
We wouldn't be able to express our feelings,
We wouldn't be able to share secrets with our friends,
We would be peaceful but wouldn't it be boring.

Hetty Jackson & Ellie Shingles (10)
Tickton CE Primary School, Beverley

Henry VIII

Large foods
Massive moods

Big boozer
Mean loser

Old dad
Young lad

Divorce king
Jewellery bling

Hat fan
Fat man

Hairy beard
Quite weird.

James Woods (9)
Tickton CE Primary School, Beverley

The Sound Collector

(Based on 'The Sound Collector' by Roger McGough)

Late this morning a stranger called,
Clothed head to foot in grey,
Every sound goes in his bag
And nothing gets in his way.

The buzzing of the strip lights,
The clicking of the car locks,
The chatter of the engineers,
The crunching of the gearbox.

The humming of the pressure pump
As it fills up a brand new tyre,
The ancient welding machine
Sets the work surface on fire.

The dripping of the oil,
The banging of the hammer,
The vibration of the radio,
The rattle from the old banger.

The ringing of the telephone
Covered in black fingerprints,
The bellowing of the manager,
'Follow my helpful hints.'

The roaring from a car engine
Keeps little children away,
The old car is towed off,
Perhaps they'll see it again someday.

Late this morning a stranger called
And took all the sounds we had,
It's so hard to live without sounds,
So this bloke is definitely bad.

Christopher Foster (10)
Tickton CE Primary School, Beverley

A Bag Of Blitz Sounds

(Based on 'The Sound Collector' by Roger McGough)

A figure shot to London,
Clothed in gas mask and cloak,
Stuffed the blitz sounds in his bag,
He was a dodgy bloke.

The wailing of the ambulance,
The sighing of the nurse,
The howling of wind,
The snigger from the curse.

The crying of the children,
The explosions of the Blitz,
The booming of the bombs
That blew my dwelling to bits.

The screaming of the sirens,
The dripping of the blood,
The wailing of the bodies,
Falling to the mud.

The crying of the citizens,
The humming from the planes,
The crackling of the fire
Coming from Pudding Lane.

The chatter from the underground,
The chuckling from the sky,
The bawling of the soldiers
Who were soon to die.

Did that figure understand,
Disaster passed him by,
There's one thing that's crystal clear,
If I could I'd cry.

Lauren Wilson (10)
Tickton CE Primary School, Beverley

The Sound Collector

(Based on 'The Sound Collector' by Roger McGough)

A stranger called at my house,
Wearing black and white,
In his bag went every sound,
He crept into the night.

The whinging of a sister,
The sneezing of a mother,
The shouting of a father,
The screaming of a brother.

The squelching of mud outside,
The whistling of the breeze,
Cutting of summer grass,
The swishing of the trees.

The beep of a mobile phone,
The humming of the fridge,
Blaring of the radio,
The creaking of the bridge.

Rumbling of the dishwasher,
The squeaking of the floor,
Turning pages of a mag,
The slamming of a door.

The rattling of a curtain,
The tweeting of the bird,
The clinking of wine glasses,
Mixing for lemon curd.

A stranger called this evening,
He took our sound off the floor,
Maybe he'll return these things
And pass them through the door.

Megan Selway (11)
Tickton CE Primary School, Beverley

The Sound Collector

(Based on 'The Sound Collector' by Roger McGough)

A stranger called this morning
At the Olympic track
He put the sounds in his sack
And wouldn't give them back.

The jumping of the people
The cheering of the crowd
The clicking of broken chairs
The spectators shouting loud.

The stab of the javelin spear
The whirring through the air
The crying of the thrower
The sounding of a flare.

The shot of the starter's gun
The scraping of the spikes
The thump of the runners' feet
And the screeching of bikes.

The clapping of the crowds' hands
The jumping on the track
The noise it makes when people pant
And when their breath won't come back.

A stranger called this morning
He didn't leave a note
Just silence all around the track
But he left without his coat.

Connor Ashby (10)
Tickton CE Primary School, Beverley

If I Were A . . .

If I were a rectangle
I could be a bestseller book waiting on a bookshelf in WH Smiths
I could be a whiteboard with lots of workings out on in a top
scientist's study
I could be a new kind of chocolate bar being tasted and tested
by a food critic
I could be a TV up on Wayne Rooney's wall

If I were a sphere
I could be a Champions League football being kicked around
by Frank Ribery in the final
I could be a tennis ball about to be served by Roger Federer
in the Wimbledon final
I could be a crystal ball being gazed into by a fortune teller
I could be a toclafane model flying around disintegrating people
in a Doctor Who who episode

If I were a star
I could be on a World Cup football in the final of the 1998 World Cup
I could be on the Australian flag wafting in the breeze
I could be Ronaldo.

Lewis Pritchard (9)
Tickton CE Primary School, Beverley

Somewhere In School Today . . .

The next Jacqueline Wilson is creating one of the best children's books.
The next Wayne Rooney is scoring the winning penalty.
The next Leona Lewis practising to get the perfect sound.
The next Christopher Columbus is planning his next adventure.
Somewhere in school today is me!

Rachel Stanforth (10)
Tickton CE Primary School, Beverley

The Sound Collector

(Based on 'The Sound Collector' by Roger McGough)

A stranger called at home,
Dressed in a hooded cloak,
In his bag went every sound,
He was a nasty bloke.

The whistle of the kettle,
The television chatting,
The dripping of the tap,
The pots and pans clattering.

The parents' moan about the bills,
The barking of our dogs,
The groan of loose floorboards,
The crackle of fire logs.

The squeak of the cupboard door,
The creak of the old bed,
The purr of our hungry cat,
The sigh of someone well fed.

Leaving us only silence,
He took all of our sound,
Life is now a misery,
I hope it can be found.

Victoria Kirbitson (11)
Tickton CE Primary School, Beverley

I Am Electricity

I am electricity . . .
The supersonic current flows through me flying high.
I have a sparkle of energy trying to escape.
A flashing feeling in my tummy ready to light a bulb.
There is a deadly light in my heart.
I feel like a filament because I am as hot as the sun.
I feel like a switch going on and off.
I am electricity . . .

Jessica Chew (8)
Tickton CE Primary School, Beverley

I Am Electricity

I am electricity . . .
The instant current zooms through me like a laser.
The rapid current shoots through me like an eagle gliding
                                              through the sky.
The complete circuit runs continuously through my arms and legs.
At the click of a switch the luminous lightbulb slowly appears
                                              in my body.
At the click of a switch I give birth to a bulb.
I whizzed down the circuit sizzling and twisting down, my body
                                              full of energy bursting out.
I can be as deadly as a fierce adder yet
I can be kind and willing.
I am electricity.

Evie Guttridge (9)
Tickton CE Primary School, Beverley

I Am Electricity

I am electricity.
The headlong current cascades through my veins.
My heart is the source of the circuit deep inside,
Transmitting needed energy through my fiery body.
At the click of a switch,
I surge with power, brightening the room.
My teeth are the forks,
travelling through the wrapped up wires.
You may think I am deadly,
but I bring you entertainment, energy and heat.
I soar high above.
You would not be here without me,
I am electricity.

Jack Head (8)
Tickton CE Primary School, Beverley

I Am Electricity

I race around your house powering nearly every object
with my crackling flames.
I stretch my power through my veins and into the lightbulb.
I run round the circuit letting my power go as fast
as a 1,000-mile-an-hour dog.
I can be as deadly as a rattlesnake scorpion with a white-hot tail
but I can protect one or another.
I gust through the socket to the outside world where I'm free to dance
through the air like a soaring bird.
I'm electricity, I flicker through the wire like a firework.
I'm electricity, I'm as deadly as a seeking scorpion looking for its prey.
I'm electricity, I power your house each and every day
and I never wear out!
My fiery furnaces work up your machines and each day I stick
to do my job, just think where you'd be without me.
But mark my lightning words do not touch me, you'll feel like
a tornado's tearing you apart.
For I am electricity.

Emily Haysom (8)
Tickton CE Primary School, Beverley

I Am Electricity

I am electricity . . .
I flow through a complete circuit.
I am as deadly as a killer whale.
I am as powerful as an engine.
As soon as a switch gets pushed I make it light.
You would not be here without me.
I bring you heat, light and energy.
I bubble and squeak with excitement.
I am the sun falling from the galaxy.
I am a dragon spearing the sky.
I am electricity.

Thomas Moran (8)
Tickton CE Primary School, Beverley

My Tudor World

I like to look at
People walking past with shimmering jewels,
Rats scurrying by like a train,
People knocking on doors like a heartbeat.

I like to listen to
Crusty bread cracking when first made,
A dagger getting thrown on the floor like a plane crashing,
Vagrants getting whipped with the whip that's like an octopus.

I like to smell
Fresh soggy clothing that has been swished in the water like a fish's tail,
Priceless perfume like sweet candy being eaten,
Golden wheat swaying like a gentle crowd listening to soft music.

I like the taste of
Fresh bread fizzing like powder from a sweet,
Thick meat that is salty like the sea,
Smoke swirling in the mouth like a tornado.

I like to touch
The lumpy tree bark like an old man's skin,
Dried leaves crumbling under my feet like a cliff side,
Bread sinking into my fingers like a worm.

Jacob Tame (8)
Tickton CE Primary School, Beverley

My Tudor World

I like to look at
Horses trotting through the streets,
Trees swaying from side to side like people waving,
Animals chasing each other in the fields.

I like to listen to
The blacksmith banging on a horse's shoe,
It is like a piece of metal being thrown from the top of the stairs,
People's footsteps stamping on the floor like an elephant charging
towards you.

I like to smell
The fresh bread from the bakers,
The smoke from the chimney like a train coming into the station,
The leather from a horse's saddle.

I like to touch
The crumbly brick from a house,
The horse's nose is like a new blanket,
The fresh crispy bread from the bakery.

I like to taste
The salted meat for my tea,
The wine from the Inn is like blood,
The fresh bread straight from the oven.

Tristan Gray (8)
Tickton CE Primary School, Beverley

My Tudor World

I like to look at
The Lord of the Manor rushing past as the farmers' wives call out
for customers,

Beggars praying madly for money,
The manor house till the lights go out.

I like to listen to
Horses galloping down the streets,
The blacksmith's hammer banging on the metal,
Birds singing madly.

I like to smell
Fresh bread flowing through the streets,
The fresh air swirling around,
Dirty ragged people that pass by.

I like the taste of
The smoke swirling into my mouth,
Fresh air blowing through my hair,
The leaves as they float past.

I like to touch
The houses as they crumble down,
Horses as they wave their heads,
The trees as their branches wave in the breeze.

Georgina Moxon (7)
Tickton CE Primary School, Beverley

My Tudor World

I like to look at
Sheep chomping the grass like lawnmowers,
Horses galloping past,
Beggars praying for money.

I like to listen to
People shouting,
Hooves clopping,
The metal being battered.

I like to smell
Smoke from the blacksmith,
Wet pine,
Wet dust.

I like the taste of
Wheat in the fields,
Cheese from the farmers' wives,
Wine from the Inn.

I like to touch
Fresh bread,
Cold stones,
Flour as it oozes through my hands.

James Wake (8)
Tickton CE Primary School, Beverley

My Tudor World

I like to look at
Hills that sit still and quiet like a huge flat in the middle of the city,
Trees waving from side to side,
Horses galloping like the speed of light.

I like to listen to
The baker chopping the bread,
The people mumbling like monkeys,
Henry VIII shouting like an elephant.

I like to smell
The perfume of the rich people walking past in the countryside,
Baker's bread when I haven't had my breakfast,
The blacksmith's smoke swirling like a tornado in a storm.

I like the taste of
The baker's bread, crusty and soft,
Fresh air tickling past my face,
Cheese from the market.

I like to touch
The grass from the jagged hills like a hairbrush tickling you,
Henry VIII's jacket wrinkled like a tiger's skin,
My hair, it feels fuzzy like a bear's fur.

Joshua Fisher (8)
Tickton CE Primary School, Beverley

The Fruits And Veg Poem!

A   is for apple, crunchy and sweet,
B   is for bananas that monkeys eat.
C   is for carrots, curvy and coloured orange,
D   is for dragon fruit which comes from a packet.
E   is for energy you get from the fruit,
F   is for fabulous figs filling the mouth with fine tastes.
G   is for gorgeous grapes, green as grass,
H   is for harvest festival, ploughing through fields.
I   is for interesting fruits that we eat,
J   is for juicy juice from juicy fruits.
K   is for kiwi fruit with a sour taste,
L   is for lemony lemons, yellow and sour
M   is for melon, tough and green
N   is for fruit that is nutritious
O   is for orange orange; sweet and sour,
P   is for passionate passion fruit.
Q   is for quantities of different fruits,
R   is for raspberry, ripe and red.
S   is for strawberry, sun-ripened and succulent,
T   is for tamarind, tender and tawny.
U   is for unique different types of fruits,
V   is for vitamins from various fruits.
W   is for wonderful watercress,
Y   is for yam, yummy and sweet.
Z   is for zesty zucchini.

Sajida Desai (9)
Wellington Primary School

Winter

W inter is soon coming and it's very cold and chilly.
 I cy and slippery on the pond.
N oses are red like cherries.
T he snow is crunching under my feet.
E yes are very sticky.
R obin Redbreast is singing a winter song.

Cherri Chan (6)
Wellington Primary School

Winter

Winter is here, I'm so cold.
Let's go to the park,
The ducks are ice skating on the pond.
Can I join in? It looks like fun.

Dewdrops like diamonds.
My nose is as red as a rose.
Fingers and toes are frozen blue.
I am so cold icicles are hanging from my nose.

Naomi Firth (7)
Wellington Primary School

Winter

Winter, winter is coming here,
'Hip hip!' I very loudly cheer.
Sparkly dewdrops hanging from the trees,
I can hear children laughing with glee.
My cheeks are as red as roses
I can see Robin Redbreast doing poses.
My little fingers are as cold as ice
But I love playing in the snow
Because it's crunchy and nice.

Jessica Banks (6)
Wellington Primary School

Winter

Winter, winter, winter, the snowflakes tumble from the sky.
I build a snowman, it's as tall as me!
His tummy's round, big and fat.
The hailstones sparkle as they crash on the snowy floor.
I throw snowballs before I go inside.
I snuggle up warm and before you know
I'm fast asleep and I'm snoring very loudly.

Aimee Johnson (6)
Wellington Primary School

Winter

Jack Frost has been.
It's icy on the path.
I am going to build a snowman.
Let's go inside and get a carrot, scarf and hat.
I need to get some stones for his mouth and eyes.
After I'm finished I am going to throw some snowballs
Before I go back inside.

Lauren Hammond (7)
Wellington Primary School

Winter

Hi, my name is Jack Frost
I am a little silly billy boy.
My name is Jack Frost because
My fingers are always covered in snow.
My tingling toes are trembling
When I walk through the snow.
I like to build snowmen
They make me feel very happy.

Ramneet Shergill (7)
Wellington Primary School

Winter

Wrap up warm. Hey! Where's my hat?
Get off it will you, silly cat!
Everybody come outside
Look at the floating flakes of snow.

It looks so frosty I think my cheeks will glow.
The happy polar bear rolling and tumbling on his own.
I saw him.
Honestly I really did!

Ashleigh Yates (7)
Wellington Primary School

Winter

Winter is here, I am full of joy and glee
I think I might go and build a snowman
When I play in the snow my cheeks go numb.
What an exciting day, I think it's time for bed.
I'd better put on my cosy pyjamas
If not I'll probably get a chill!

Holly Byrne (7)
Wellington Primary School

Winter

Winter, winter, winter is coming!
Autumn's ending and winter's starting!
The flowers begin to go away and
Fall into their winter sleep.
The robin redbreast flies around
Looking for berries on the ground.

Jasmine Jackson (7)
Wellington Primary School

A Trip To The Zoo

My mum and dad thought about me and you.
So they booked a holiday but first we went to the zoo.
We ended up there at quarter past two.
We lost our ticket, we didn't know what to do.
But then we quickly rushed through.
When we got to the farm we saw some cows.
They all got together and went, 'Moo!'

Arun Singh Atwal (7)
Wellington Primary School

My Cat

My cat is lazy.
She sleeps all day
And doesn't like milk.
I play and tease her
When she purrs on my knee.
I love my cat.

Shannon Drake (8)
Wellington Primary School

Rocket

5, 4, 3, 2, 1, take-off,
The fastest rocket ever,
Shooting into space,
Flying past Mars, then
Bang!
The rocket crashes into the moon.

Joseph Newell (8)
Wellington Primary School

Love And Hate

Love is red like raspberries in a bowl
It tastes like sweet meringue with cream,
It smells like hot sponge cake,
It looks like a bursting heart with roses blooming
It sounds like the sweet songs you've ever heard,
It feels like bursting laughter.

Hate is dark blue waves crashing,
It tastes likes mouths full of onions,
It smells like burning toast,
It looks like mourners and a graveyard,
It sounds like a kettle whistling,
It feels like being outside in a storm.

Georgia Caitlin Pickles (9)
Wellington Primary School

Love And Hate

Love is red like a beating heart,
It tastes like fresh strawberries with rich melted chocolate,
It smells like fudge cake baking in the oven,
It looks like freshly picked roses,
It sounds like a romantic song,
It feels like floating in the deep blue sea.

Hate is black like clouds full of rain,
It tastes like burnt toast,
It smells like choking smoke,
It looks like a hideous green monster,
It sounds like shouting in your ear,
It feels like being trapped in a black hole.

Hannah Swift (8)
Wellington Primary School

Hate And Love

Hate is as red as thick blood,
It tastes like raw meat,
It smells like the withered stench of cabbage,
It looks like someone boxing at your face,
It sounds like loud music blaring through car windows,
Hate feels like your nails rubbing on dry sandpaper.

Love is as red as a rose,
It tastes like fresh picked strawberries,
It smells like sweet smelling perfume,
It looks like a gorgeous Valentine's card being given,
It sounds like a lovely choir singing,
Love feels like being lifted up and flying through the air.

Abigail Leeming (8)
Wellington Primary School

Happiness And Sadness

Happiness is green like freshly mown grass,
it tastes like warm apple pie with custard at the side,
It smells like popcorn popping in warm butter,
It looks like red roses with tall straight stems,
It sounds like little children singing nursery rhymes,
It feels like being tucked up cosy in bed.

Sadness is blue like tears running down your face,
It tastes like the juice from sour lemons,
It smells like dead animals on the road,
It looks like ghosts hovering round you,
It sounds like an air raid siren screaming at you,
It feels like being outside on a snowy night.

Brandon Doherty (9)
Wellington Primary School

Happiness

Happiness is blue like the afternoon sky,
It tastes like sweet raspberries with a teaspoon of sugar,
It looks like a class full of smiley faces,
It smells like lavender in a wood full of animals,
It feels like having a hot chocolate next to the fireplace,
It sounds like a lawnmower going over the grass.

It looks like the waves crashing on the rocks,
It tastes like an orange smoothie waiting to be eaten.
Happiness is yellow like the burning sun,
It smells like a cake baking in the oven,
It feels like taking a walk in the countryside,
It sounds like birds singing melodies in a nest.
Happiness is what makes the world go round.

Leah Fowler (8)
Wellington Primary School

Pain And Recovery

Pain is red like sickly blood oozing,
It tastes like sour milk in a glass,
It smells like sweaty socks in boots,
It looks like a volcano erupting,
It sounds like a tap constantly dripping,
It feels like an almighty electric shock.

Recovery is white like the hospital itself,
It tastes sweet like hot apple pie,
It smells like chocolate cake in the oven,
It looks like the shoots of new growth in spring,
It sounds like the laughing of young children,
It feels warm like the sound on the beach.

Morgan Green (8)
Wellington Primary School

Happiness And Sadness

Happiness is colourful like a rainbow,
It tastes like sweet oranges with rich cream,
It smells like a sponge cake cooking in the oven,
It looks like a garden of red roses,
It sounds like seagulls flying over the sea,
It feels like white snow falling from the sky.

Sadness is black like being stuck in a hole,
It tastes like sour milk,
It smells like mouldy blue cheese,
It looks like ghosts coming to get you,
It sounds like howling winds blowing against you,
It feels like crashing thunder overhead.

Molly Joyce (9)
Wellington Primary School

Happiness And Sadness

Happiness is yellow like the burning sun,
It tastes like strawberries with lashings of cream,
It smells sweet like chocolate cake baking in the oven,
It looks like a vase of raspberry tulips on the window sill,
It sounds like birds singing sweet melodies,
It feels like being warm in front of a roaring fire.

Sadness is blue like smashing waves of the sea,
It tastes like a gulp of sour fruit pop,
It smells like mouldy wood on the forest floor,
It looks like sad mourners at a funeral,
It sounds like thunder rolling across grey skies,
It feels like being out on a cold winter's day.

Josef Musgrove (9)
Wellington Primary School

Pain And Recovery

Pain is black like midnight sky,
It tastes like blood running down your throat,
It smells like burning smoke,
It looks like people in agony,
It sounds like shouting in your ear,
It feels like being run over by a truck.

Recovery is pink like the sunrise,
It tastes like ripe banana split,
It smells like a cake in the oven,
It looks like a field of wheat ripening,
It sounds like the crying of a newborn baby.

Callum Churm (9)
Wellington Primary School

The Journey Of A River

Spring sprouter
Canyon crawler
Rapid roller
Cliff braver
Dam buster
Trench digger
Meander rider
Tributary catcher
Habitat holder
Sun glistener
Toe tickler
Sea searcher.

Siân Wilkinson (11)
Wellington Primary School

I Wish I Was A Shark, Like Shark Boy

I love sharks
They're big and strong
So many different kinds
To swim along.

But watch out for
Their razor teeth
They eat anything
That they meet.

I would love to dive in the sea
To watch the sharks
Swim around me.

I love the great white shark
And hope one day to see
One to swim along by its side
In the great blue sea
Maybe at The Deep.

Mitchel Cooper (8)
Wellington Primary School

Teachers And Friends

Healthy Halliwell, my best teacher,
Intelligent Illingworth, the best assistant teacher,
Desirable Dixon, our unit co-ordinator,
Smiley Slater, a Year 4 teacher.

Happy Hannah, my first best friend,
Running Rebecca, my second best friend,
Talented Tilly, my third best friend,
Silly Sophia, Talented Tilly's best friend,
Super Sally, who sits opposite to me!

Very healthy Hannah! (That's me!)

Hannah Scowby (7)
Wellington Primary School

The Months

Jolly January, a new year
Funky February, foggy and Valentine's
Marching March, spring flowers appear
Awesome April showers fall
Magical May, Easter bunnies run by
Jumbo June, playing out, having fun
Jolly July, lots of fun
Anxious August, goes on holiday
Super September, move up class, try and make new friends
Naughty November, bonfire night and fireworks
Dancing December, Santa comes and gives you presents
Christmas dinner.

James William Street (7)
Wellington Primary School

Fox's Night Out

Dear Chickens,

Stay in tonight
Fox's going to give you a fright.
I advise you not to go out late
He'll be ready to exterminate.
His big soft bushy tail
Ready to cut with his sharp nail.
Big white teeth like a knife,
Those sharp things will cost you your life.
Killing thing all the time
I think it should be a crime.
So young chickens stay in your shed,
Is it worth losing your head?

Umayr Hanif (10)
Wellington Primary School

Months Of The Year

Jolly January, a new year.
Fantastic February full of joy.
Marvellous March magic comes.
Ace April showers fall.
Magnificent May sun starts to come out.
Joyful June water guns out and children shout.
Jumping July adults sunbathe.
Amazing August, people by the seaside.
Super September, sun goes down.
Ordinary October, Hallowe'en comes with screams from every house.
Nasty November has nippy weather.
Dark December with Christmas dinners.

Meg Lenehan (9)
Wellington Primary School

Dolphins

I have a dolphin that lives in my pocket
it fits around my neck rather like a locket.

My dolphin splashes in the sea
it puts on its trunks and goes for a swim in the sea.

After it's had a bath it flips and splashes all over me
in the afternoon it has chips for its tea and says it loves me.

Flipper, my dolphin and I go to the sea
every morning or maybe after tea.

Sally Clegg (8)
Wellington Primary School

Paint

I was sitting at the table, thinking what to do,
then suddenly I knew.
I can paint a picture and a special one as well,
with birds, flowers and a tree
and maybe just maybe a little buzzy bee
and I can paint a hill
and a hard-working mill.
I can paint a fox creeping all about,
I can paint a river, with a jumping trout.
I can paint a yellow sun shining here and there,
I can paint some children dancing everywhere.
I will paint a picture with green and red and blue
and at the bottom I will write, this if from me to you.

Rosie Shackleton (9)
Wellington Primary School

Chocolate, Chocolate

Chocolate, chocolate, have a try
After that you'll want to buy.

Every time I try that taste
No bite, no crumb goes to waste.

Inside, outside, not a care
I eat chocolate everywhere.

Chocolate, chocolate, ever so sweet
Chocolate, chocolate, that's mine to eat.

The nicest taste that you've ever found
Will only cost about a pound.

Chocolate, chocolate, oh so yummy
Chocolate, chocolate in my tummy.

Kate Banks (11)
Wellington Primary School

The Bogeyman

Down the road on a cobbled street
In a house and up the stairs
You see a cupboard opening
Alone you see a hand so black.
it can burn your face to smithereens
He's a little tiny guy.
You think he's harmless
You think he's nice,
Oh I forgot to tell you his name.
Don't run to me if you have bad dreams.
Now his name is the bogeyman *eek! Argh!*

Liam Harrison (8)
Wellington Primary School

One Snowy Day

This morning I woke up,
no school today.
Then I saw the snow,
hip hip hooray.
I put on my coat,
my gloves, hat and scarf.
I went out with my friends,
we had a good laugh.
The snow was so cold
it made me shiver and shake.
We made lots of snowballs
and patterns with my rake.
I had a good time,
I know it won't last.
I'll make the most of it
because it well melt fast.

Owen Ryan Tate (8)
Wellington Primary School

Cricket

Cork ball coming fast
Right-handed batsmen coming to the crease
Is the match slipping from their grasp?
Catches now will be vital
Kicking the ground in frustration
Everyone on their feet for the final delivery
Time is up, Yellows victorious.

Jamie Woodhouse (10)
Wellington Primary School

Winter

W inter is here, it's freezing cold.
 I 'm feeling, I'm feeling really, really bold.
 N oses are freezing and are as bright as a rose.
 T he snow is crunching, crunching under my toes.
 E xcited today, the snow is tumbling.
 R udolph's nose is as red as a rose
 A nd so are ours because we're out in the snow.

Esha Sagar (7)
Wellington Primary School

Winter

Winter has come the snow is soft and cold.
I run outside. Boy it's freezing!
Noses brighter than Rudolph's.
The bare branches are covered with snow.
Eyes feeling very stinging.
Rabbit's fur covered with frost.

Sam Karpov (7)
Wellington Primary School

Young Writers Information

We hope you have enjoyed reading this book - and that you will continue to enjoy it in the coming years.

If you like reading and writing poetry drop us a line, or give us a call, and we'll send you a free information pack.

Alternatively if you would like to order further copies of this book or any of our other titles, then please give us a call or log onto our website at www.youngwriters.co.uk

Young Writers Information
Remus House
Coltsfoot Drive
Peterborough
PE2 9JX

(01733) 890066